THORPE ST. .

A History

TREVOR NUTHALL

Thorpe St Andrew - A History
First Published 2002 by

Trevor Nuthall
7 Rectory Court
Elm Grove Lane
Norwich NR3 3LH

ISBN 0-9543359-0-2

Typeset & printed by Catton Print of Norwich

CONTENTS

Page

III: From the Present and Old Churches to Barber Place

IV: From 103 Yarmouth Road to School Avenue

V: From Thorpe Mews to Primrose Crescent

VI: From Pound Lane to the Griffin

LIST OF ILLUSTRATIONS AND MAPS

Page

Plates

Page

Maps (drawn by Brian Larkman)

INTRODUCTION

Outline

This book outlines briefly where Thorpe St Andrew is and its relationship with the original parish of Thorpe-next-Norwich or Thorpe Episcopi. The history of Thorpe is then traced by describing an imaginary two-mile journey along Yarmouth Road from Harvey Lane to Boundary Lane (just beyond St Andrew's Park). Many of the buildings and lanes along the way are described and linked with the historical development of Thorpe, concentrating in the main on Thorpe before 1850, but including some information about later buildings. Finally, in the appendices, the story of the lordship of the manor of Thorpe is told, there are maps of Thorpe in about 1600 and about 1750 and details are given of the sources used in compiling this history.

Something about the history of Thorpe before 1500 can be found in "The Original Church and Settlement", "Thorpe Hall - Description and early history" and the "Red Lion". The major changes that happened in the 16th century are picked up in "The Old Church and the Movement of the Settlement". The history and development of Thorpe Hall and St Andrew's Hospital are described in detail. (St Andrew's Hospital is now "St Andrew's Park" and "St Andrew's Business Park"). There are also descriptions of the three churches of Thorpe St Andrew ("the present church", "the old church" and "the original church"). Also described are the green, common, public houses, poorhouses and all significant buildings that stand or have stood along Yarmouth Road between Harvey Lane and Boundary Lane. In addition, the story of Yarmouth Road itself has been traced as well as that of the lanes and tracks that link or have linked with it, including Yarmouth Way.

Many sources have been used but particularly significant have been maps, especially:-
a map of Mousehold Heath of 1585 ("the 1585 Mousehold map");
a map of Mousehold Heath of about 1600, showing sheepwalks ("the 1600 Mousehold map" - the Thorpe St Andrew section of this is reproduced as Plate 31 in Appendix 2);
two sketch maps of between 1700 and 1731 ("the 1700 / 1731 sketch maps");

an 1825 map of rivers between Norwich and Reedham, with names of owners of adjacent lands ("the 1825 river map");
the 1841 tithe map for Thorpe ("the 1841 tithe map") and
Ordnance Survey maps of the 1880s and later.

Use has been made of information in the Norfolk Sites and Monuments Record maintained by Norfolk Landscape Archaeology at Gressenhall.

Details of all sources used are listed in Appendix 3.

Where is Thorpe?

Thorpe St Andrew has only been the official name of the parish since 1954. Previously it was known as Thorpe-next-Norwich and, prior to 1536, as Thorpe Episcopi or Bishop's Thorpe.

Since Norwich expanded in the 15th or 16th century, Thorpe has been a divided parish. It has been split between the part of Thorpe in Norwich (Thorpe Hamlet) and the part of Thorpe in Broadland (now known as Thorpe St Andrew). The dividing line is Harvey Lane. To the west is the city. To the east is the county.

Thorpe Hamlet is defined by the River Wensum to the west and south and Harvey Lane and a line just east of Frogs Hall Lane (east of 129 Thorpe Road) to the east. The official southern boundary of Mousehold Heath ("Chestnut Avenue" or "Beech Drive" - not far south of Gurney Road) forms the northern boundary.

The northern limit of Thorpe St Andrew runs along Plumstead Road East and the southern edge of the Greenborough Road area. (Until 1950 it went as far north as what is now Rider Haggard Road and Lishman Road on the Heartsease Estate). To the east are the parishes of Plumstead and Postwick and here the boundary runs from Green Lane North (off Plumstead Road East) to Boundary Lane (off Yarmouth Road). To the south the River Yare is the boundary. To the west Thorpe St Andrew meets Thorpe Hamlet.

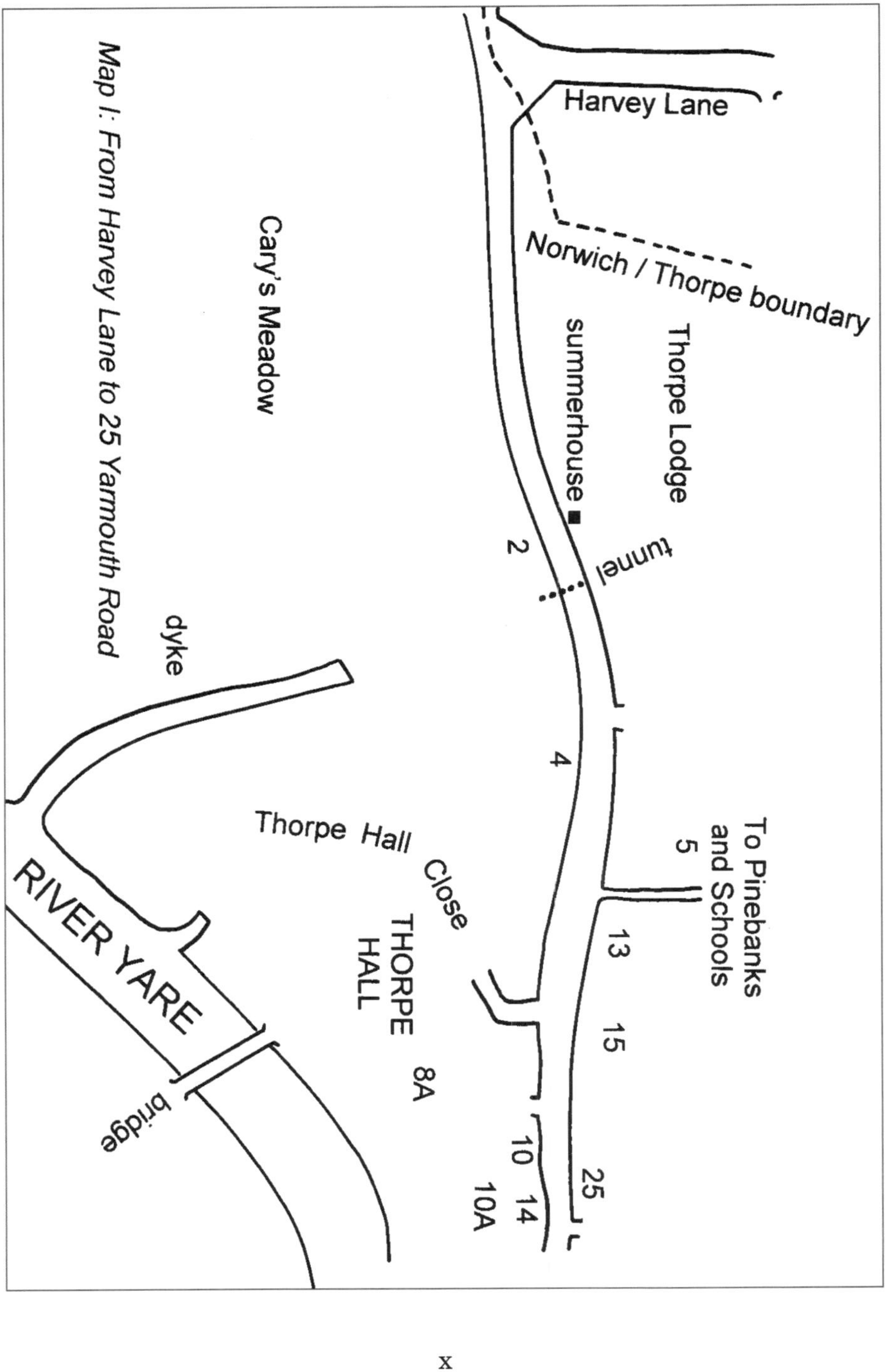

Map I: From Harvey Lane to 25 Yarmouth Road

Yarmouth Road, Thorpe St Andrew

I: From Harvey Lane to 25 Yarmouth Road

HARVEY LANE

Harvey Lane is named after John Harvey who lived at Thorpe Lodge during the first half of the 19th century (see "Thorpe Lodge" below). By the 15th century it was the boundary line between Thorpe and Norwich. A draft Norwich charter of 1461 mentions a boundary cross that stood where Yarmouth Way crossed Harvey Lane. This was by the present junction with White Farm Lane.

As well as the boundary line between Thorpe and Norwich, in the 15th and 16th centuries, Harvey Lane was the eastern boundary of Thorpe Wood. A Norwich charter of 1556 refers to it being at the east end of Thorpe Wood. A draft charter of 1461 may also imply that this was the case at that time. However, it appears that in the 13th century Thorpe Wood may have stretched as far east as Dale's Loke / Bishop's Close (see "Thorpe Hall - Description and early history" below).

Until 1801, Harvey Lane entered Mousehold Heath where the southern boundaries of the gardens of Gordon Avenue are. As late as the 1840s, it was referred to as Rose's Lane, presumably after the Rose family who owned property in Thorpe in the early 18th century. The will of Matthew Rose senior of Thorpe was proved in 1707.

In the early 19th century, the southern end of Harvey Lane was moved westwards to enable John Harvey to extend the grounds around Thorpe Lodge (see "Thorpe Lodge" below). It meant that this part of the road no longer followed Norwich's eastern boundary.

THORPE LODGE

NOW BROADLAND DISTRICT COUNCIL OFFICES

Thorpe Lodge dates from about 1800 and has five bays with sashes. Until at least the 1920s it had two and a half (rather than two) storeys and a three bay east wing that made the building symmetrical (Plate 1). It was built by John Harvey, who moved from Norwich to Thorpe in about 1800. He was a banker and textile manufacturer and had been mayor of Norwich in 1792. Harvey introduced the manufacture of shawls into Norwich in 1791. He was prominent in the local militia and was known as Colonel Harvey.

The 1600 Mousehold map shows that there had been a house on the site from at least that date. A 1767 manor court entry describes the site boundaries. To the north was the bottom of a hill called the Common Hill or the Sugar Loaf Hill. To the east was the Pound Close otherwise called the Claypit Close, belonging to the lord of the manor. To the south was the highway (Yarmouth Road). To the west was Rose's Lane (see "Harvey Lane" above).

Plate 1 : Thorpe Lodge in 1924, from a sale catalogue, showing the building before it was altered.

In 1806 Harvey acquired the Thorpe Hall estate from his father in law, Sir Roger Kerrison. Harvey extended the grounds of Thorpe Lodge to the west and to the south, possibly in 1808. He did this by diverting Yarmouth Road southwards (as far as the summerhouse opposite 2 Yarmouth Road) and Harvey Lane westwards. An 1824 Norwich map shows the old roads running south and then west along the Norwich boundary. Following the extension of his grounds, Harvey built the "crinkle crankle" wall that now runs from near the bottom of Harvey Lane to where Eden Close joins Harvey Lane.

In 1833 Robberds described how in 1808 the "large fir trees" of Thorpe Wood (which he called "Thorpe Old Grove") were cut down. Looking back to the early 19th century, Hardy described how Harvey had "bought the whole of Thorpe Grove, enlarged the Park about his own house, built a house with grounds for his second son, and by the mere sale of timber on the estate, reimbursed himself for the price paid." (Harvey's second son was George Harvey. Part of his house, "The Grove", may now be incorporated in the house of that name that adjoins 4 Matlock Road, off Thorpe Road).

Harvey was involved in property development and the replanning of Thorpe Hamlet following the building of Carrow Bridge and Foundry Bridge in 1810. This included creating the part of Thorpe Road from Foundry Bridge to the junction with Rosary Road and making a road from Carrow Bridge (then at the bottom of Carrow Hill) to Thorpe Road.

Harvey's father, Robert, died in 1816 and left him property in Lingwood and Blofield. It was bequeathed on the basis that Harvey had a life interest and on his death it would pass to his children or to such of them as Harvey decided. In May 1818 Harvey secured a private Act of Parliament, under which these trusts were transferred from the property in Lingwood and Blofield to the Thorpe Hall estate, including Thorpe Wood (by then known as Layne Wood). Over the next twenty years, Harvey divided the Thorpe Hall estate between three of his children. Sir Robert John Harvey, his eldest son, was given most of the land west of Harvey Lane. (Here he built what became Mousehold House). Harriot Blakiston, Harvey's sixth daughter, was given Thorpe Hall (see "Thorpe Hall – Thorpe Hall from 1536" below). The rest was given to Roger Kerrison Harvey, Harvey's third son.

South-east of Thorpe Lodge and opposite 2 Yarmouth Road is an octagonal summerhouse that Harvey built. The 17th century door-frame that used to contain the door to the road is mentioned below in connection with Thorpe Hall. By 1841 Harvey had adapted the summerhouse as a camera obscura. This was a darkened chamber into which light was admitted through a double convex forming an image of external objects on paper or glass placed at the focus of the lens.

About 27 yards (25 metres) east of the summerhouse, there is a tunnel running under the road. It is an underground passage between Thorpe Lodge and Thorpe Hall that is now a cave for bats. In 1842 it was described as leading "from the Lawn to the Gardener's Cottage, and Kitchen Garden" (Thorpe Lodge), "to the premises of the Home Farm, and the Boat-houses near the river"(Thorpe Hall). It is a tunnel folly faced with flint and brick and constructed by John Harvey following the fashion of the time. It was refaced in the 1920s.

In a July 1841 account of a bazaar in the grounds of Thorpe Lodge, it was observed that the "tunnel which leads down to the meadows was a source of attraction – it was lighted with coloured lamps and had a novel appearance." Reference is also made to "the greenhouses, conservatories and camera

Plate 2 : Outside the gates of Thorpe Lodge, looking up Yarmouth Road, in about 1910.

obscura" in the grounds of Thorpe Lodge. Grigor, writing in the same year, also refers to a "grotto, beautifully secluded among the trees".

In Norwich Castle Museum & Art Gallery there is a large painting called *Thorpe Water Frolic - afternoon*. It is by Joseph Stannard and was first exhibited in 1825. Harvey had instigated the water frolic in 1821 partly as a sporting event but more importantly as a social event for the gentry. It was repeated in 1822 when cutters and rowing boats raced for silver cups. In 1823 the event was opened up to the working population of Norwich and the local weavers were given a holiday. 10,000 attended in 1823 and nearly twice that number in 1824. There were clear social distinctions. The gentry amused themselves on the north bank of the river (the Thorpe side) and the working population on the south bank (the Trowse side).

Fawcett describes Stannard's painting:-
"On the left, enclosing Harvey himself, are the members of his family, his guests and the Dragoon Guards band; the ladies show off their fine fashionable dresses and bonnets, the gentlemen wear or flourish top hats. On the right, at the inner bend of the river, are the ordinary citizens, more or less displaying the traits of popular manners."

The event was repeated several times during the 1820s and revived in 1835. There were similar regattas in the 1840s (organised by Robert Cattermole of Thorpe Gardens - now the Rushcutters) and also in the 1850s.

BETWEEN THORPE LODGE AND 25 YARMOUTH ROAD

The oldest building between Thorpe Lodge and 25 Yarmouth Road may be 13 Yarmouth Road (Ivy Cottage). At the time of the Harvey sale in 1842, it included "Wheelwright's, Carpenter's and Blacksmith's shops, Sawpit-house" and "Timber Yard". It does not appear on the 1825 river map. The Sites and Monuments Record describes it as an early 19th century flint cottage with brick quoins, window surrounds and a string course at the level of the upper floor. There is a blocked window over the door and one original chimney pot. Map evidence suggests that 15 Yarmouth Road (Inglehurst) also dates from about the 1830s. In 1842 it was called Vine Cottage.

West of 13 Yarmouth Road is a track that may mark what was the eastern boundary of the Thorpe Lodge estate. Before Harvey extended the estate westwards, the boundary was probably opposite the eastern boundary of 2 Yarmouth Road. (This is where Harvey's tunnel goes under the road – see "Thorpe Lodge" above). The estate was encroached upon in about 1850

Plate 3 : Looking down Yarmouth Road from the site of 2 Yarmouth Road, in about 1910.

by Holly Lodge (5 Yarmouth Road) and in about 1860 by Sunny Hill (now 7 Yarmouth Road). Sunny Hill was first associated with William H. Clabburn, a shawl manufacturer. In the early 1950s Thorpe House School moved there (see also "Old Thorpe House" below). Most of the original building was demolished in the 1970s.

Before reaching Thorpe House School, the track forks eastwards towards a large house that dates from about 1880. In 1880 it was known as Belle Vue, a name that was changed in about 1900 to Beech Hill. It was first associated with Hugh Gurney Barclay, a banker. It is now Langley Preparatory School, 11 Yarmouth Road.

For Pinebanks (9 Yarmouth Road), see "School Lane and Pinebanks" below.

THORPE HALL

Description and early history

On the south side of Yarmouth Road is Thorpe Hall.

In 1735/36 Harrison described Thorpe Hall as "encompassed with a flint Stone Wall." This implies the wall went right round the site. From the eastern edge of Cary's Meadow, you can see what is left of the flint wall that runs along the east side of the 147 yard (134 metre) dyke or ditch, immediately west of 16-25 Thorpe Hall Close. This was the western boundary of the site. The dyke may have been dug as a moat and may have once extended along the whole of the western side of the hall.

The boundary on the southern side of the site was the river, although there is some evidence of a wall along it, perhaps chiefly as a defence against flooding. An 1818 drawing of Thorpe Hall (Higham) (Plate 6) shows a ruined wall south-east of the present hall and running west-south-westwards about 20 yards (18 metres) from the river. The garden walls that in the 1880s ran in the same direction up to a second dyke and then up to the 147 yard (134 metre) dyke (Plate 4) may originally have been continuations of this wall. They started south of the house about 20 yards (18 metres) from the river and joined the western wall referred to above about 60 yards (55 metres) from the river.

The eastern boundary of the site probably ran between what are now 14 and 12 Yarmouth Road. The latter is known as the Manor House (see "12 Yarmouth Road" below). Part of the northern half of the present wall between the properties (immediately east of what is now 10A Yarmouth Road) may contain parts of the original wall that encircled Thorpe Hall.

Much of the original northern boundary of the site can be seen in the brick and flint wall that forms the present boundary along Yarmouth Road. The original boundary wall may have run from near the eastern boundary of 2 Yarmouth Road to the boundary between 14 and 12 Yarmouth Road. There may have been some angling northwards of the boundary between just east of a point opposite what is now 13 Yarmouth Road and 14 Yarmouth Road. This is suggested by the change of angle of the wall east of the garden entrance and the old masonry that has been built into it just before Thorpe Hall Close. In addition, it is clear from the manor court records that in 1744 part of this boundary was extended seven yards (six metres) northwards to include what is now 14 Yarmouth Road. In the 1980s, the wall was affected by the building of Thorpe Hall Close and the new access to Thorpe Hall. The latter is in about the same place as an access to the hall that was there by 1825.

Until 1841 the principal entrance to Thorpe Hall was opposite what is now the modern extension to Thorpe Lodge. From the 1880s Ordnance Survey map (Plate 4), it is clear there was a track that came in here (across the present site of the Anglian Water pumping station) curving south-eastwards and then eastwards. It would have entered the manor site, north of the 147 yard (134 metre) dyke referred to above. Entry may originally have been through a gateway and would have been into an outer court. To the north were farm buildings and to the south were fishponds. In the 1880s, when you entered the outer court, you would have seen to the north a large barn

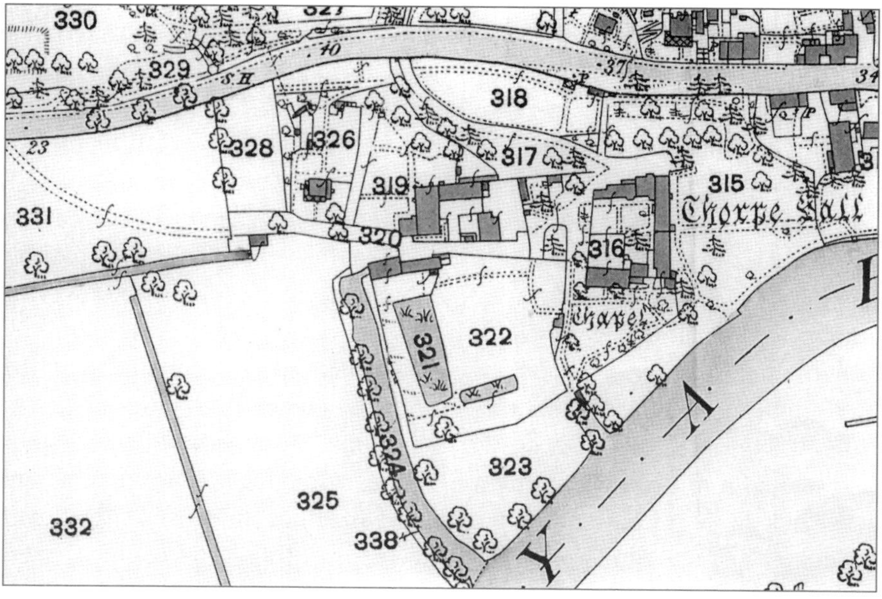

Plate 4 : Thorpe Hall from the Ordnance Survey 25 inch map of the 1880s.

and then a stable and to the south pigsties and, behind them, east of the dyke, two fishponds. There were three fishponds in 1825, but the third had been filled in by 1841. Parts of the barn were believed to be medieval.

Continuing eastwards beyond the barn yard and stable yard, you would have entered what could be regarded as the inner court. To enter it, you would have crossed a boundary that included the second dyke, which in 1841 was about 67 yards (61 metres) in length, but by the 1880s had been shortened considerably. (What remains of the dyke now seems to be between 14 and 15 Thorpe Hall Close). As you entered the court, there were buildings on three sides. This is an area occupied today partly by the hall and partly by the property immediately south-west of it (7-12 Thorpe Hall Close). Now the only part of the hall that remains is the south wing and part of the west wing. In the 1880s, the south wing would have had a low southern extension that ran down towards the river, thus forming the eastern side of the courtyard. (The southern extension would have run up to the current southern boundary of Thorpe Hall). East of the end of that extension, and forming the southern side of the courtyard was the chapel. (Its site is now outside the current boundary of Thorpe Hall. It is immediately north of 13 Thorpe Hall Close and partly under 7-12 Thorpe Hall Close). In the 1880s, the low west wing would have continued a little further with a taller extension at it western end. It formed the northern boundary of the yard.

From what can be ascertained from the building, Thorpe Hall may have been a 14th century courtyard house. What is now the south wing comprised, from south to north:- opposing doorways (forming a screens passage), an open hall (with a chimney on the western side that still exists) and a parlour (with rooms above). The southern extension would have contained service rooms for the storage and preparation of food. An architectural survey suggests that the present west wing of the hall did not originally join the south wing. Until the 1950s or the 1960s the present low west wing was 50% longer again than it is now. The missing western third had a higher and steeper roof than what remains. It appears that the difference in height was because of a fire that badly damaged much of the west wing. It was rebuilt with a much lower roof. This makes its difficult to imagine what it was originally like. The west wing may have contained service rooms.

According to Kent, the chapel on the south side of the yard had five Decorated windows, a fine cross on its western gable, a stone piscina and two finely moulded doors. The mouldings on the doors agreed very closely with the door in the north wall of Suckling House, Norwich, to which a date of between 1350 and 1370 was given in 1917. The chapel was demolished in 1936 (Plate 5). In 1958 the doors were said to be at Sudeley Hall in Gloucestershire. The east gable cross of Fritton church in Suffolk is said to have come from Thorpe Hall, presumably from the chapel.

A 1535 survey (Supple pages 72-3) describes the hall as the "fermour's dwellynge, with a stable annexed to it at the west end; and with two barns and pigstyes at the end of them, with the kyl-house" (i.e. a malt-kiln). In 1428/9 10s 10d was spent on a new great table and nearly £5 on roofing the bake-house and hall (Hayes).

The hall was a multi-purpose building. It was primarily a farm run by the bishop's bailiff to provide income and produce for the bishop and his household. It was also the manor house of Thorpe, where the bishop or his officials held the manor court. Other official business was also undertaken

Plate 5 : Thorpe Hall chapel, being demolished in 1936.

there, including the issuing of charters. The earliest charter issued at Thorpe dates from 1206, although at that time the hall may have occupied a different site (see below). In the early 15th century some heresy trials were held at the hall either in the chapel or in the parlour (Tanner). Sometimes the bishop stayed there. According to Hayes, it was Bishop Alnwick's favourite residence in the Norwich area. In 1425 Bishop Wakering died in the house.

Thorpe Hall, as we see it today, probably dates from the 14th century. There may have been a manor house on the site in the 13th century, but exactly where is not clear. Supple (page 60) refers to there being "considerable foundations". Kent said "some early foundations had been found but never explored". It may have been a timber-framed building without any stone foundations.

Yaxley and Virgoe have suggested that many manor houses are some distance from the original focus point of the settlement, because they were established in the 12th or 13th centuries, when new parts of the parish were being brought into intensive cultivation. They mention Colkirk, "where by 1296 the manor house had been removed from the centre of the village to a moated site on the edge of a large area of heath and woodland nearly a mile to the east of the parish church." All these factors may well have been true at Thorpe, although the manor house may not have moved until the 14th century.

Harper-Bill (139) quotes an agreement of 1239 under which the part of Thorpe Wood covered with oaks was divided equally between the Bishop of Norwich and the Cathedral Priory. The bishop was granted the half nearer his manor. The priory was granted the half nearer Bishop Bridge. An undated "book of measurement" of Thorpe Wood is written in the handwriting style of the 14th or 15th century. It was made between the bishop and the priory and describes how the main wood covered an area of more than 155 acres. In terms of size, this equates with what was shown as "Thorpe Wood" on the 1600 Mousehold map i.e. an area west of Harvey Lane, south of Yarmouth Way and north of Rosary Road / Thorpe Road. At the time of the 1239 agreement, the dividing line between the wood granted to the bishop and that granted to the prior may have been what are now Wellesley Avenue South and the track that runs northwards to Wellesley Avenue North. If so, the part of the wood granted to the bishop may have stretched from this line as far east as the original line of School Lane (see "School Lane and Pinebanks" below). However, it is more likely that the eastern limit was Dale's Loke / Bishop's Close (see "The Original Church and Settlement" below).

The part of the wood east of Harvey Lane was probably cleared for cultivation in the 13th or 14th century. Thorpe Hall may have been built as the focus of this new agricultural area. It is now clear that it was about a mile from the original church (see "The Original Church and Settlement" below). It is likely that the earlier manor house would have been much closer to the original church. (However, it is possible that, at least in the 12th century, the Bishop's Palace in Norwich served as Thorpe's manor house. It was built at the end of the 11th century on land that Cathedral Priory records suggest may then have been part of the manor of Thorpe).

In 1735/6 Harrison referred to "a Chappel belonging to the Hall, the remains whereof converted into a Barn, stand upon an eminence opposite to it on the other side of the Street". This building was clearly on the north side of the road, but its exact location and function are not clear. It is possible, but unlikely, that it was an earlier manor house site. There is no other indication that there was a chapel in this vicinity. Although evidence is slight, the most likely site of the building is what is now 27 Yarmouth Road – a site truncated by road-widening in 1956 (see "Between 25 Yarmouth Road and School Lane" below). If so, it was opposite 12 and 16 Yarmouth Road. There were cottages on the site by 1800 and nothing by 1841, when it had become the garden of the property adjoining it to the east – part of the Brew Yard estate. It may have been the building called the "Stonehouse" that was acquired by Thomas Vere in 1747, 14 years after he acquired the property on the opposite side of the road (i.e. 12 and 16 Yarmouth Road).

Thorpe Hall from 1536

By the early 16th century the hall and parts of the manor estate were let to various tenants. For example, in 1534 the Bishop of Norwich let the hall, 84 acres of arable land ("demesne and decayed land") and about 11 acres of meadow to Ralph Cantrell, Ann his wife and Thomas their son. Ralph Cantrell received 40 shillings a year as keeper of the manor of Thorpe and 20 shillings a year as bailiff of the manor. He paid rent of £7 0s 7d. Although manor courts would continue to have been held at Thorpe Hall, it was principally a farm-house.

A major change to Thorpe Hall happened in the 1590s. Edward Paston had inherited the estate from his father shortly after Edward was born in 1550. Edward married his second wife, Margaret Berney, in the 1580s. In the 1590s he embarked on a series of building campaigns. Brett suggests that he began with Thorpe Hall in about 1590. He then moved on to Binham, where work was abandoned because of a fatal accident. In 1596/7, work

Plate 6 : Thorpe Hall, from a drawing by T Higham of about 1818.

started on what was to become his principal residence - Appleton Hall, near King's Lynn. In 1612, he built a further hall at Barningham, near Holt.

At Thorpe Hall, Paston remodelled and partly rebuilt the hall. What you can see on the east front of the south wing is largely Paston's work. He made new window openings in the medieval walls, floored the hall and perhaps heightened the building. He also seems to have joined the south and west wings by the addition of a staircase hall. The mainly moulded brick, mullioned and transomed windows with pediments date from this rebuild.

Edward's building work on Thorpe Hall may have been planned as a celebration of his marriage to Margaret Berney. In what may have been the parlour at the north end of the south wing, he put a stone fireplace. (In the 1840s this became the dining room). It included the arms of his father, Sir Thomas Paston, impaling the arms of his mother, Ann Leigh, and his own arms impaling those of his wife. The same arms were put on a stone chimney piece in what would have been the hall in the southern half of the south wing. (In the 1840s this became the kitchen).

Edward, a Catholic, turned the house into a cultural centre for the quiet pursuit of music and poetry and built up a large library. It is known from the Norwich Mayor's Court Books that the Earl of Essex's players performed at Thorpe in June 1585. This is likely to have been at Thorpe Hall. It is unlikely that Edward Paston ever resided regularly at Thorpe, though it is clear from his will that he kept a number of books of music in his study there. Correspondence of Lady Katherine Paston of 1603-1627 includes a letter of January 1624 in which Edward wrote that he would go to Thorpe on the first day of the next Sessions. He was at Thorpe at the end of May 1624. He had been there at the end of July 1611.

Edward died in 1630 and the property passed to his grandson Clement, also a Catholic. It may have been Clement's principal house. When the Civil War began in 1642, Clement's land was sequestered which meant that all income and profits went to Parliament and its soldiers. The manor was released from sequestration in 1656 and Clement sold it to Revd. Nathan Wright, a Norwich prebend. A valuation of about 1670 shows that by then the hall had been divided, "the south end of the hall place, the plowman's stable and other houses" having been let to Robert Gimber.

The Manor House (12 Yarmouth Road) dates from the 17th century. It was built outside (but next to) the walled site of Thorpe Hall. In 1733 Thomas Vere purchased it and appears to have lived there. He is important in the history of Thorpe Hall, because, although he purchased the manor of Thorpe in 1751, he does not appear to have moved to Thorpe Hall, but chose to continue to live at the Manor House / Walpole House. Although the names "the Manor House" and "Walpole House" are not recorded until the Harvey sale of 1842, in the enclosure survey of 1800 Thorpe Hall was referred to as "Thorpe Old Hall". This was presumably in contrast with the much more fashionable Manor House / Walpole House. The name "Manor House" may have arisen because Vere lived there while lord of the manor. Vere's fellow MP for Norwich was Horatio Walpole and the name "Walpole House" may have been a tribute to him.

Although the centre of attention had probably moved to the Manor House / Walpole House by say 1730, Thorpe Hall was not neglected. In about 1700 there was some further remodelling. Some rectangular windows were inserted. These can be seen in the west wall of the south wing. It may have been while Thomas Vere was lord of the manor that the large barn that is now 10A Yarmouth Road was built. According to notes in the Sites and Monuments Record, the fire that destroyed much of the west wing happened in the 18th century. No record of this event has been found.

When, in 1806, John Harvey acquired the estate attaching to the manor, he did not choose to live at Thorpe Hall. He was developing his own residence at Thorpe Lodge on the other side of the road. However, he did make some changes to the hall. In particular he probably introduced some Tudor and Jacobean doorways from his family properties in Norwich. This was in line with the growing popularity of antiquarianism. Until about 1970, there was a doorway in the garden entrance to Thorpe Hall, opposite 13 Yarmouth Road. In its left-hand spandrel was the merchant mark of Silvester Force, a worsted weaver of St George Colegate. In the other spandrel was the date "1583", which has sometimes mistakenly been regarded as the date of the hall rather than the date of the doorway. Until 1977, on the other side of the road, was another doorway. This was in the octagonal summerhouse opposite 2 Yarmouth Road. In the spandrels were the Grocers' arms and the merchant's mark of George Cock, who was mayor in 1613 and lived in Bacon's House, Colegate, from where the door was taken.

There may have been two George Cock doorways at Thorpe Hall. A 17th century doorway was clumsily inserted into the east front of the south wing. It had the initial G in one spandrel and a cock in the other. In addition, there was a door in the short west wing with the date 1608 in a spandrel. According to Ewing, "1608" is the date associated with Cock on a panel and in doorways at Bacon's House.

Comparing Higham's drawing of the hall in about 1818 (Plate 6) with the 1825 river map, it seems that between these years, Harvey altered the grounds on the east side of hall. Walls were demolished or cut back and the area of lawn in front of the house was reduced in size. The purpose was to create a track along the boundary between the hall and what is now 10 Yarmouth

Plate 7 : Thorpe Hall, from a drawing by James Stark of about 1829.

Road. The track broadened considerably near the river, taking in the river frontages of what are now 10 and 14 Yarmouth Road, resulting in a frontage of about 80 yards (73 metres). The purpose may have been to provide a viewing area for spectators at the regatta or "water frolic" that Harvey began in 1821 (see "Thorpe Lodge" above). This new track can be seen in James Stark's "*Thorpe Old Hall, Norwich*", that dates from 1829 (Plate 7).

In 1838 Harvey gave the hall, with five acres of land, to his sixth daughter, Harriot, who eleven years previously had married Captain Thomas Blakiston, R.N. This was the first time that the hall had gone into separate ownership from the farm buildings to the west. In 1841/42, the Blakistons restored, decorated and adapted the hall and grounds for their own use. A new porch was added to the short west wing and a low passage was added to provide access to the west wing. A new main entrance from Yarmouth Road was built. (This now leads to 4 Yarmouth Road). It bears the arms of Harvey (including three crescents) and Blakiston (including three cocks). A new drive was constructed from the new entrance to the hall. The track that Harvey had created between the hall and 10 Yarmouth Road was taken back into the enlarged lawn of the hall.

The hall remained in the ownership of the Blakistons and their successors, the Cubitts, until 1929. In 1930 it came into the hands of a boat-builder, Alfred G Ward. He erected two boat-sheds on the river bank in the southern part of the site. In 1936 the chapel was demolished to make way for an engine repair shop. A few years later, the low extension to the south wing was pulled down. In the 1940s, after the Second World War, 4 Yarmouth Road was built. In the 1950s or the 1960s the tall extension at the end of the west wing was demolished. In the early 1960s, Alfred Ward sold his part of the property to Jenners of Thorpe, boat hirers, apart from a site east of the hall where he built a bungalow (8A Yarmouth Road). In the 1960s Jenners built the concrete bridge across the river, south of hall, as a part of plans to develop a marina complex on the other side of the river. In the early 1970s, Thorpe Hall was sold and the farm buildings were pulled down. They included a farm bungalow north of the principal dyke. In the 1970s vandals set to work on the hall. At the same time, the dining-room panelling and stone fireplace surrounds were stolen. Following a campaign, the hall was saved and restored in the 1980s and Thorpe Hall Close was built.

10 AND 14 YARMOUTH ROAD

Map evidence suggests that 10 Yarmouth Road dates from between 1825 and 1841 and that 14 Yarmouth Road ("Manor Cottage") was built between 1841 and the 1880s. No. 10 seems to have replaced a range of presumably farm buildings that backed on to Yarmouth Road. No. 14 appears to have replaced a coach-house and stables that were on the northern end of what is now 10A Yarmouth Road (formerly a barn).

According to manor court records, in 1744, the coach-house was extended northwards seven yards (six metres) beyond what would have been the Thorpe Hall boundary, taking in part of "the waste of the manor". The consequent movement northwards of the road has been referred to above in "Thorpe Hall - Description and early history".

Until the early 1900s there was a pump at the roadside nearly opposite the road that now leads to Pinebanks and the Thorpe House and Langley schools. The pump was not far from the small garden entrance to Thorpe Hall. It may have been a parish pump, at least for this part of Thorpe.

Plate 8 : Yarmouth Road looking towards Thorpe Narrows, and, on the right, rough ground outside Thorpe Hall with 10 and 14 Yarmouth Road beyond, in about 1910.

The pump may have been on a narrow village green that ran along the side of the road and the only surviving remnant of which is the lay-by outside the old roadside boundary wall of Thorpe Hall (Plate 8). It was encroached upon during the 18th century, and possibly earlier, by the tenants of Thorpe Hall moving and rebuilding the boundary wall between the pump and what is now the main entrance to the hall. The sites of the buildings now called 10 and 14 Yarmouth Road may have previously been part of the green. However, the only direct evidence concerns the site of 14 Yarmouth Road for which a licence to enclose "the waste" was obtained from the manor court in 1744.

25 YARMOUTH ROAD
FORMERLY THE STORK NURSING HOME AND SITE OF THE ORIGINAL GRIFFEN

This is on the opposite side of the road to 14 Yarmouth Road. It is an interesting building. Until the Harvey sale in 1842, the site was part of the manor estate. The present main building may encase an earlier building that was there by 1825. The eastern extension had been added by 1841. By 1725 and until at least 1800 it was the site of the Griffin public house. (In 1800, west of it, was a blacksmith's shop).

The public house had moved to another site by 1825. In 1842, the building that remained was described as "Two Dwelling-Houses, Brick and Tile built, called "Griffin Cottage"." It can be seen on a lithograph of Thorpe from the railway of about 1850 (Cotman and Hawcroft page 12).

Between 1825 and 1841 the building was extended eastwards. Limestone blocks can be seen in the flint side-wall of the extension. The blocks could

Plate 9 : The Gables (now 25 Yarmouth Road) and, on the right, 10 and 14 Yarmouth Road, in about 1905.

have come from the building that had previously stood on the site of what is now 27 Yarmouth Road (see "Thorpe Hall - Description and early history" above).

Between the 1880s and 1907, the main building was either rebuilt or recased (Plate 9). The gables of the new building no longer extended as far as the road and the section between the gables was brought forward. The building was re-roofed and given decorative Tudor-style chimneys. The eastern extension was given a brick façade to the road.

A griffin was the badge of the Pastons who were lords of the manor of Thorpe from 1547 to 1656. Their coat of arms included six fleurs-de-lis. A fleur-de-lis and two griffins (sitting, collared and with wings back to back) can be seen in each of the gables of the building.

As already mentioned, by 1825 the Griffin public house had moved to a site east of asylum (see "St Andrew's Park" below). In 1846 it moved to its present site, west of the asylum.

By the early 20th century, "Griffin Cottage" had become known as "the Gables". It later became the Stork Nursing Home.

It appears from the 1600 Mousehold map (Plate 31 in Appendix 2) that the eastern boundary of the Griffin was the eastern boundary of "Thorpe several". The "several's" western boundary was approximately the line of Harvey Lane. "Thorpe several" appears to have been the part of Thorpe Wood that, following clearance in the 13th or 14th century, was taken into the Bishop of Norwich's estate (see "Thorpe Hall - Description and early history" above). By the 16th century it was pasture left open to Mousehold Heath.

Immediately south of the Griffin's eastern boundary is the boundary between 14 and 12 Yarmouth Road. This is the eastern limit of the Thorpe Hall site.

II: From 12 Yarmouth Road (the Manor House) to 53 Yarmouth Road

12 YARMOUTH ROAD (THE MANOR HOUSE) AND 16 YARMOUTH ROAD (WALPOLE HOUSE)

On the opposite side of the road to No. 25 and next to No. 14 are the Manor House (No. 12) and Walpole House (No. 16) (Plate 10). The origin of these houses has already been mentioned in "Thorpe Hall – Thorpe Hall from 1536" above.

The Manor House dates from about the middle of the 17th century. The south façade to the Manor House was added in about 1700. In about 1730 Walpole House was added as a pavilion to the Manor House. In about 1750 the houses began to be treated as separate dwellings. This division did not become permanent until the middle of the 19th century. In the late 18th or early 19th century, northern additions were made to both houses.

Plate 10 : View across the river showing Walpole House (No.16), 18 and 20 Yarmouth Road and Town House, probably in the 1890s.

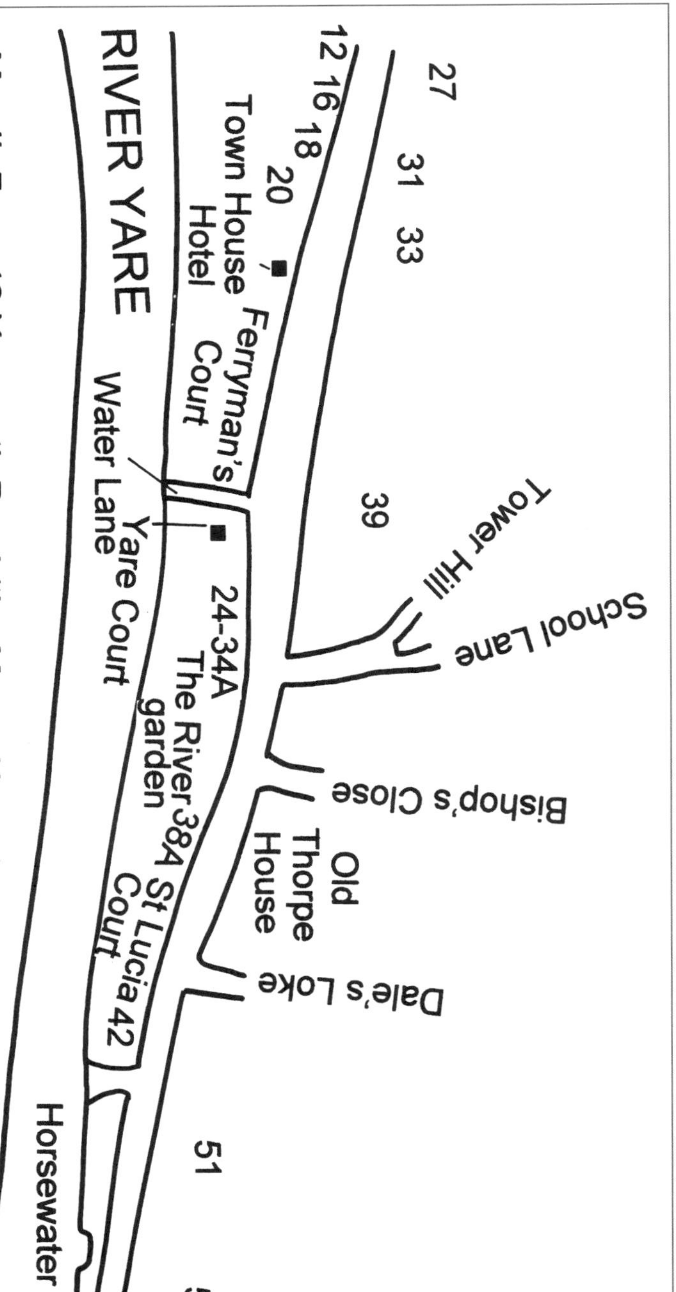

Map II: From 12 Yarmouth Road (the Manor House) to 53 Yarmouth Road

The northern addition to the Manor House is now divided between "Well Cottage" and "Manor Lodge".

According to the Sites and Monuments Record, the main east-west block of the Manor House has an external north stack and, in the north wall, blocked large openings on each of the two floor levels, with possible traces of a timber frame. The southern façade of the building is in two sections, one of four bays between rusticated quoins and the other of three bays with a moulded stringcourse.

The original part of Walpole House has three and a half small bell gables protruding above the roof on both its north and south sides; the easternmost of these having been cut in half. They can be seen in Joseph Stannard's *Thorpe Water Frolic – afternoon*, first exhibited in 1825.

South of Walpole House is a garden-house of mid-18th century date, square, with a door, sash window, oriel window and internal stack. The roof is a pyramid. There is internal panelling and a seascape painted over the fireplace. There seems to have been a link between the Manor House and the barn, coach-house and stables referred to above in connection with 14 Yarmouth Road. When the Manor House was sold in 1842, the purchaser was granted an option to purchase them.

Two owner-occupiers of the Manor House/Walpole House seem to have been Elizabeth Coulson and Thomas Vere.

Elizabeth Coulson is buried at St Andrew's church, Norwich. She died in 1732 at Thorpe, probably in this house, aged 88. She was the daughter of John Man, mayor of Norwich in 1653 and described as "the richest man in the town". Elizabeth appears to have acquired the property in 1698 and is recorded as living in Thorpe in 1700. She was the older sister of Mary Chapman, who was the wife of Samuel Chapman, rector of Thorpe from 1670 until his death in 1700. It is probable that, following her husband's death, Mary Chapman lived with her sister Elizabeth in this house until Mary died in 1724. Mary is famous as the founder in 1713 of the Bethel Hospital in Norwich. Her memorial stone in Thorpe church records that she built it "wholly at her own expense ...for the reception, maintenance and cure of poor lunaticks". She gave her inheritance from her father, all her income and her estate to the charity she had founded.

On her death in 1732, Elizabeth Coulson bequeathed the Manor House to her granddaughter, Elizabeth Skottow. In the following year, she sold it to Thomas Vere. It was probably at this time that the older part of what is now Walpole House was built as a pavilion to the existing house. Vere, a worsted manufacturer, was mayor of Norwich in 1735. In the same year, he was elected as a Member of Parliament for Norwich, an office he held until 1747. In 1751, Vere purchased the lordship of the manor of Thorpe. In 1755 Vere presented gifts to Thorpe church. According to a note in the parish register, he gave "a set of Silver Communion Plate in a Mahogany Case with Silver Handles, Hinges and Escutcheons, containing Two Flaggons, one Cup, one Waiter, one receiver for the Arms (sic) and a Knife with a Silver Handle. He also erected at his own expense a new Altar-Piece, new floor'd, repaired and painted the seats and beautified" the church. In the same year, he "built a new Schoolroom upon the Town Ground adjoining the Church House" (see "Ferryman's Court" below). In 1766, he died, aged 85. Vere's son, John, does not appear to have lived in Thorpe. He died childless in 1790 and his father's property passed to his father's "much esteemed Friend", Thomas Lobb Chute of South Pickenham.

18 AND 20 YARMOUTH ROAD

Structurally, this is one building but originally it was two houses. Its north façade to the street is of seven bays, but the central bay is false, screening the partition wall and central stack.

According to the Sites and Monuments Record, Edmund Cotman, father of the "Norwich School" artist John Sell Cotman, purchased one of the houses (No.18) in 1820, probably when it was newly-built. On 3 November 1841 John Sell Cotman visited his father there and did a preliminary study for his painting "*From My Father's House at Thorpe*". It was a modest house of two sitting-rooms, four bedrooms and a kitchen. Edmund Cotman was still living there in 1842 when the freehold was sold in the Harvey sale. At that time No. 18 and No. 20 were referred to as "London House". Edmund Cotman died in 1843.

There is no evidence that John Sell Cotman ever lived in this house or anywhere else in Thorpe. However, according to Moore, his two sons, John Joseph Cotman and Miles Edmund Cotman, also artists, did live in Thorpe between 1849 and 1855. According to the 1851 census, John Joseph Cotman lived close to the Buck (see below), possibly immediately north or north east of it.

18 and 20 Yarmouth Road are now part of the Town House Hotel. They were not the first buildings on the site. There was a house there in 1800 and, according to manor court records, had been since at least 1728.

TOWN HOUSE HOTEL AND BEEFEATER RESTAURANT

FORMERLY TOWN HOUSE

Like the southern façade of the Manor House, this building dates from about 1700.

The Sites and Monuments Record (SMR) describes it as having "two storeys, the ground floor acting as basement" on the south façade "owing to the slope of the hill".

The SMR goes on to say:-

"The north facade is much altered and painted over. The basement windows have been blocked. The south façade has had the ground floor walling removed for a modern extension; the upper level is of five bays in red brick set between rusticated brick quoins... Beyond the east quoins is an extra bay...the brickwork however appears identical. To the east of this are two 20th century additions, infilling a service court, and then another building.... perhaps a stable or coach house."

There has been much confusion over the name of this building. It was probably called "Town House" not because it was ever a poorhouse or belonged to the parish but because it adjoined land that belonged to the parish and where the Church House (also known as the Town House – see "Ferryman's Court" below) originally stood.

By 1800 it was occupied by Peter Columbine Esq. and was described as "a capital messuage (formerly three tenements)." By 1825 it was occupied by Thomas Davey and by 1886 by George James Newbegin. Newbegin was a Fellow of the Royal Astronomical Society. He installed a powerful telescope in the garden. By 1916 the property had passed to Ernest Curl, a department store owner. It was later in the hands of George Jenner, who founded his boating business there.

BETWEEN 25 YARMOUTH ROAD AND SCHOOL LANE

On the other side of the road, between 25 Yarmouth Road and School Lane, there is a range of modern buildings that date from the 1960s. The buildings that used to be there were demolished as part of a road-widening scheme in 1956.

Between 18/20 Yarmouth Road and School Lane a new road was built north of the old one. The old road was closed at both ends and became a service road for the houses on the southern side. Between School Lane and 51 Yarmouth Road, Yarmouth Road was widened on its northern side. This involved the demolition of houses at the southern end of School Lane (Plate 12), a reduction in the size of the gardens in front of Thorpe House and 51 Yarmouth Road and the demolition of the Guild Cottages that were near the western boundary of No. 51.

This stretch of road had been known as "Thorpe Narrows", because it was only 15 feet (4.5 metres) wide in places, and yet it was part of the main road between Norwich and Yarmouth.

A dramatic consequence of the road widening was the demolition of the buildings between 25 Yarmouth Road and School Lane. 27 Yarmouth Road (an office building) has been mentioned above in "Thorpe Hall - Description and early history". On the site and in front of what is now 29 Yarmouth Road (an office building) and the western quarter of a block of flats called "Conrad Court" (33 Yarmouth Road), there was a group of buildings that in 1842 were referred to as "Brew Yard Estate" (Plate 11). They were opposite what are now 18/20 Yarmouth Road and the western half of the Town House Hotel. In 1842 they consisted of a house, a bakery, seven cottages, a chaise-house, a stable and a large warehouse. Most of the buildings were on the roadside, but the cottages were within Brew Yard. The entry to the yard was opposite where 18/20 Yarmouth Road joins Town House Hotel. The name "Brew Yard" suggests that there may have been a malt-house here in the late 18th or early 19th century. No reference to it has been found. The buildings fronting the street may have been there in 1800.

East of the "Brew Yard Estate" and on the site and in front of most of what is now Conrad Court was another group of buildings. It was opposite what is now the car park east of the Town House Hotel and the western end of Ferryman's Court. Near the street were a house and a butcher's shop. Behind them, in 1842, were a barn, stable, cart-lodge, slaughterhouse, piggeries and enclosed yards. Immediately east of these buildings and fronting the street were a house and shop with a plumber's shop at the back. This group of buildings seems to have been erected between 1825 and 1841.

Further east and on the site and in front of what is now a petrol station and shop (39 Yarmouth Road), there were two adjoining houses that, in 1842, were called "Holley Wood". They had shrubberies, a garden, a stable and a chaise-house. The western half of the house was later known as "Hollywood Cottage" and the eastern half "Honeysuckle Cottage". The house was opposite Water Lane. There appears to have been a building on the site in 1800. Behind this house and the buildings described in the previous paragraph was a chalk and marl pit (see "School Lane and Pinebanks" below).

Plate 11 : On the left is Brew Yard, just before demolition in 1956.

FERRYMAN'S COURT

THE SITE OF CHURCH HOUSE AND VERE'S SCHOOL

On the other side of the road to Conrad Court is Ferryman's Court. Although it is a modern development, the land where it stands is of historical interest.

In 1587 the area of land between what is now the Town House Hotel and Water Lane (and including the car park east of the Town House Hotel) was given to the parish by Byrford Lath and Thomas Walker on certain conditions. The land (and any buildings on it) were to be let and the rent applied towards repair of the church and other parish charges. The land was known as "freblod" or "the Rose Ground" and had a river frontage of 61 yards (56 metres). Until about 1760 the site was commonly known as the Town Land because it belonged to the parish.

Two important buildings stood here. The first was a row of five small thatched cottages built in the 16th or 17th century and known until 1760 as the Town House and from then until their demolition in about 1890 as the Church House. (The reason for the change of name was to distinguish them from the poorhouse that was built in a different part of the parish). The five cottages are shown on a lithograph of Thorpe from the railway of about 1850 (Cotman and Hawcroft page 12). They were built close to Yarmouth Road and Water Lane.

In 1755 Thomas Vere decided to build a new schoolroom for the parish. It was erected as a western extension to the cottages. Vere's school replaced an earlier charity school (site unknown) founded in 1700 by Revd Samuel Chapman and said in 1709 to be "where 12 poor children were taught to read". In 1839 the Charity Commissioners reported that the schoolmaster at Vere's school taught 12 children in reading and the church catechism and attended with them every Sunday at the church. Two of the scholars were also taught writing. The children were all nominated by the rector. The master was then 70 years of age, and scarcely competent to teach. He was assisted however by his daughter who kept a "pay school" in the dwelling-house, which he rented. The school remained in use until 1841 when a new school was opened on School Lane and the old school was pulled down.

In 1888 the Trustees of the Church House sold the land. Shortly afterwards, the cottages were demolished. In the 1950s the site was occupied by Jenners' boat-sheds. It is now occupied by modern flats - Ferryman's Court - and a car park.

From the 1861 census, it appears that "Thorpe Street" was the part of Yarmouth Road between the cottages on the site of Ferryman's Court and Thunder Lane.

WATER LANE

It has been established that this is a public right of way. In 1587 it was referred to as a common lane. In 1716 it was known as Watering Lane or Water Lane. From 1767 it has been known simply as Water Lane. "Watering Lane" suggests it was a place where animals were brought to drink. The 1841 tithe map describes it as a "landing place" i.e. a place where goods were landed from the river.

Although it is not altogether clear, it may be Water Lane that is shown in Joseph Stannard's *Thorpe, Near Norwich* of about 1820 (see Moore, page 99). If so, it shows a more complicated pattern of buildings on the other side of Yarmouth Road than is evident from the 1825 river map.

Water Lane now runs under the western end of Yare Court.

BETWEEN WATER LANE AND THE RIVERGARDEN (FORMERLY THE KING'S HEAD)

Between Water Lane and the Rivergarden are (1) modern flats (Yare Court) and a pair of Edwardian semi-detached houses (24 and 26 Yarmouth Road), (2) two large Victorian houses (28 and 30 Yarmouth Road) and (3) a smaller Victorian building and a 1930s(?) engineering works (32, 34 and 34A Yarmouth Road). From at least the mid-18th century these were three separate tenements. (Where the western extension to 28 Yarmouth Road now is used to be part of the first tenement).

In 1829 the tenements were briefly united when a large house was built on what was the second tenement and its gardens extended across the other two tenements. In 1842 it was described as a "capital Dwelling-house". It had a "large walled-in Garden, between the house and the river, with a terrace walk of fifty yards (46 metres) next the latter". There was also a stable and chaise-house and a gardener's cottage. By 1842 the cottage had been converted into a laundry. However, by the 1880s the house and garden had gone and there were three separate tenements again.

Plate 12 : On the left are 45, 47 and 49 Yarmouth Road and the garden wall of Thorpe House, just before they were demolished in 1956.

SCHOOL LANE AND PINEBANKS

On the other side of the road is School Lane.

The cottages on the right appear from the date-stone to have been built in 1867 by Donald Dalrymple. At that time, he was living at Thorpe Lodge. The cottages replaced a cottage, blacksmith's shop and warehouse that were here by 1841. When Yarmouth Road was widened in 1956, the first of the cottages, 1 School Lane, was demolished, as was 45 Yarmouth Road that adjoined it (Plate 12).

Beyond the cottages is an old school. The original school was built in 1841 and consisted of a large room 40 feet (12 metres) by 12 feet (3.5 metres) with a door, into the lane, at the west end. The basis of this large room can be seen in the centre of the present building. An incised tablet lists the names of the original subscribers and trustees. In 1855 the school was enlarged and in 1872 a large schoolroom was added. An infants' school, with its own entrance, was added in 1899. The buildings continued in use as schools until they were superseded by new schools in Hillside Avenue, in 1937, and St William's Way, in 1952.

School Lane originated as a north-south track between what is now Yarmouth Road and what was, until 1801, Yarmouth Way. It was a track between the river and Mousehold Heath. Until it was diverted in 1953, School Lane met what had been Yarmouth Way near where buildings now stand in the north-west corner of a playing field just south of Henby Way. (Part of the present School Lane runs southwards from White Farm Lane to Pinebanks. If this continued southwards as far as the end of the Pinebanks buildings, it seems from the 1600 Mousehold map (Plate 31 in Appendix 2) that it would equate with a lane that ran between "Thorpe several" to the west (see "25 Yarmouth Road" above) and "Thorpe Closes" to the east).

From School Lane to about 100 yards (91 metres) east of South Avenue, there is an accessible band of chalk running about 50 yards (46 metres) northwards from Yarmouth Road. This has resulted in the digging of chalk and marl pits since at least the early 18th century. In the Rye Manuscripts at the Norfolk Record Office, there is a Counsel's Opinion of 1757 advising that marl and lime chalk had been dug in this part of Thorpe "for a great length of time". Evidence of pits can be seen on the western side of Tower Hill, between Tower Hill and School Lane, at the top of Chapel Lane, and a short distance east of South Avenue. According to Marshall and Young, in the late 18th century, white marl was being transported by river from Thorpe to Woodbastwick, Ludham, Thrigby, Hembsy, and Langley. It was laid on the land to improve its productivity. At Langley, they laid 12 loads per acre at 4s 6d a load from the keel or barge. Tower Hill may have developed as a way into the pit. (In the 1861 census it was referred to as Marl Pit Lane). The pit between Tower Hill and School Lane is a pit within a pit or quarry. The same has happened with the pit at the end of Chapel Lane

Since 1953, School Lane has led to Pinebanks (9 Yarmouth Road). This is now Norwich Union's sports and leisure centre. The building dates from about 1880. John Odin Howard Taylor built it. He was a Norwich solicitor, a minor poet and a famous chess player. The house was known as Pine Banks Tower, because of the brick and flint tower that was built next to it. According to Rye, it was also known as "Taylor's Folly".

In 1883 the tower was used for a charity chess tournament. In 1887 Queen Kapiolani of Hawaii visited it. She was in Britain to attend the celebration of Queen Victoria's Golden Jubilee. An inscription on the tower reads: "HM Kapiolani ascended this tower June 6th 1887. Quis enim." On the other side of the tower is a quotation from Horace "Omne tulit punctuam qui miscuit utile et dulci" which translates as "He has gained every point who has mixed profit with pleasure".

In 1890 Taylor died and Pinebanks passed through various hands. In 1919 Thomas Jarrold bought it and in 1953 Norwich Union purchased it.

THE RIVERGARDEN
FORMERLY THE KING'S HEAD

On the other side of the road is the Rivergarden (Plate 12). The earliest part of the present buildings may date from the 17th century. It is L-shaped and is in the north west quarter of the plot. It is of flint and brick and has a steep-pitched, hipped roof. There are three arched windows facing the road. It returns along the western edge of the plot with a shaped gable towards the river. All the other older buildings appear to be 19th century. The northern end of the 17th century building seems to have been "recased" at the same time.

The 1825 river map shows that, at that time, there were what were probably outbuildings in the north east quarter of the plot, forming what may have been a stable yard. They may have included the steep-pitched rubble and pantile eastern extension of the present buildings. The end of this extension marks what was the eastern extent of the plot.

There was an open space, probably a lawn or bowling green, in the southern half of the plot. A pencil drawing of 1806 by John Crome -*View from the King's Head Gardens at Thorpe* (see Clifford, Plate 73) - shows several men sitting or standing under a covered arbour or box on the western side of the lawn.

By 1841 all the buildings in the north east quarter of the plot (apart from the eastern extension referred to above) had gone and most of the 19th century additions had been made. This meant that, from the roadside, the Kings Head looked much as it does today. One difference was that at the end of the eastern extension, there was another building that ran down to the river. This had gone by the1880s and was replaced by a covered arbour on the eastern side of the lawn.

The fall in the ground means that what are single storey buildings from the roadside are two storey buildings from the south. The south front has been much altered.

The building was known as the King's Head from at least 1700, when John Bunting is recorded as living there. In 1767 the land from Water Lane up to and including the King's Head was in same ownership, although with different tenants. This was still the case in 1825 but had changed by 1841. In April 2000 the name of the King's Head was changed to the Rivergarden.

OLD THORPE HOUSE
FORMERLY THORPE HOUSE

On the other side of the road is "Old Thorpe House". This dates from the late 17th century. The section of this date is at the front of the building. The building was extended northwards in about 1730. Evidence of this comes from a brick dated 1732. At the same time as this extension, the southern façade of the house was altered. Western and eastern extensions were added to the house between 1825 and 1841. When the building was surveyed in 1962, some late 17th century panelling remained and there was a portion of 18th century stair-rail in the attic. In the oldest part of the house were some ovolo moulded beams. The house has incorporated earlier doorways. Until recently, it included a grand 16th century doorway with a four-centred arch and deeply carved panels depicting leaves, fruit and fish between curving folds. By 1993 the house included a fine Jacobean door with figures on one side and a coat of arms on the other, bearing a faint name that seemed to be Ballantyne. Most of the 19th century additions to the building have now gone, apart from the western extension to the main house.

Old Thorpe House is between Bishop's Close to the west and Dale's Loke to the east. What is now the northern half of Bishop's Close used to be a continuation of Dale's Loke. In 1741 the manor court said that the then owner of the house, William Payne, could block an ancient footway running up the west side of his property from what is now Yarmouth Road up to what was, until 1801, Yarmouth Way. There was a condition. He was required to make a new footway up to the said way on the east side of his house. This suggests that Dale's Loke originated as an 18th century track up to Yarmouth Way, but, before 1741, it ran up the west rather than the east side of the house.

From about 1840 until his death in 1864, Charles Weston, a Norwich brewer, owned Thorpe House. From 1897 until the early 1950s, it was run as private school. Until 1946 it was known as Thorpe High School. It then became Thorpe House School. In the early 1950s, the school moved to its present premises – originally a house called "Sunny Hill" – south-west of Pinebanks (see "Between Thorpe Lodge and 25 Yarmouth Road" above).

In 1841 Grigor noted that at the edge of the river opposite Thorpe House, there was "a celebrated tree of the white willow, of magnitude sufficient to have induced some person to take advantage of it in building a shed, of which it forms an end. This tree is well-known to all the villagers, and they reckon no picture of Thorpe complete without it."

Plate 13 : View across the river to the Foundry (now 38A Yarmouth Road) in about 1910.

38A YARMOUTH ROAD

THE SITE OF A FOUNDRY

On the other side of the road, after the Rivergarden, is 38A Yarmouth Road. Historically, the plot where it stands ran from the end of the eastward extension of the Rivergarden to the end of the 19th century building that is now 38A Yarmouth Road.

Now, the western half of the plot does not contain any buildings. However, by 1825 there were cottages along both the eastern and western halves of the street frontage with a staithe behind. By the 1880s there were buildings behind as well as on the street frontage. On the western side of the plot was a single storey building running down to the river. On the eastern side of the plot there were smaller buildings and a yard that was entered through what is now the garage of 38A Yarmouth Road. Together these buildings formed a foundry that had been built in the 1860s (Plate 13). An 1868 directory refers to the occupier, Thomas Sabberton, as an "engineer, iron and brass founder, boiler maker and general smith and coal merchant". This was the same Thomas Sabberton who had previously been a blacksmith in School Lane. The foundry was still operating in 1907 but had been demolished by 1926. In 1954 38A Yarmouth Road became Foundry House and in 1961 Foundry House Hotel. In 1961 the hotel amalgamated with the Santa Lucia Hotel and a new building (since demolished) was erected behind it, near the river.

1-4 ST LUCIA COURT

FORMERLY SANTA LUCIA HOTEL AND ON THE SITE OF THE MAID'S HEAD

The four-gabled building that is now 1-4 St Lucia Court was until a few years ago the Santa Lucia Hotel. It was built between 1864 and 1871, as part of a complete redevelopment of the site. In 1881 it was referred to as "The Villa" and in 1901 as "Shamrock Villa".

Before it was redeveloped, the plot had been 23½ yards (21.5 metres) wide on the riverside and had been divided by a track that went down to the river as a continuation of what is now Dale's Loke. There were cottages on either side of the track as well as a cottage on the roadside. The cottage on the west side of the track appears to have been a building that in 1800 was described as the Maid's Head public house. It appears in a painting of c.1814-1817 by John Thirtle called *Cottage by the River at Thorpe, Norwich* (Plate 14 – see also Allthorpe-Guyton, Plate 4b, No. 42). By 1841, the building had been demolished although the cottages on the roadside and on the east side of the track remained until the 1864/1871 redevelopment.

(Norwich Castle Museum & Art Gallery)

Plate 14 : "Cottage by the River at Thorpe, Norwich" by John Thirtle, between 1814 and 1817, showing the way up from the river past the Maid's Head public house, in the foreground, and, in the distance, Thorpe House.

42 YARMOUTH ROAD

POINT HOUSE

This building was being constructed in 1864 when it was referred to as "The River Side Villa Residence (at present unfinished)". It had been owned by Charles Weston (see "Old Thorpe House" above). Following his death, his properties were sold by auction and are listed in the Norfolk Chronicle of 30 July 1864. When Point House was built, it replaced a double-gabled cottage on the riverside and a cottage that faced what is now Horsewater. The riverside cottage was a popular subject for artists of the Norwich School. John Thirtle's painting *Old Waterside Cottages* dates from c.1814-1817 (see Rajnai). John Crome's *On the Yare* has been dated to c.1812-1814 (see Clifford, Plate 121a).

51 YARMOUTH ROAD
GUILD HOUSE

On the other side of the road is 51 Yarmouth Road. The house dates from the late 18th century. From at least 1845 (White's Norfolk Directory), it has been known as the Guild House. The Sites and Monuments Record refers to its "pedimented doorway between two unequally projecting wings with bay windows and modillion eaves cornice". It is of brick with a slate and pantile roof.

Near its western boundary were the Guild Cottages. They were demolished by road-widening in 1956 (see " Between 25 Yarmouth Road and School Lane" above).

HORSEWATER AND THE WATERING PLACE

Opposite 51 Yarmouth Road is "Horsewater". This was the western edge of the village green (see "River Green" below). Until about 1800, the green stretched unenclosed from here eastwards to what was the edge of Thorpe Gardens (now the wall of the public toilets near what is now the Rushcutters). Almost all of the green was regarded as a place where copyhold tenants of the manor had the right to water their horses and cattle. A survey of 1767 divided the green into three sections from west to east. First there were 276 yards (252 metres) of "The Watering Place", then 19½ yards (18 metres) of Town Land and then a further 35 yards (32 metres) of "The Watering Place".

By the early 19th century the right to water horses and cattle was being associated with particular areas of the green. There were two watering places. The first was where Horsewater is now. The second was a few yards further east opposite what is now the boundary between the 51 and 53 Yarmouth Road. The first of these is shown (somewhat imaginatively) in John Joseph Cotman's *Thorpe Watering*, painted in 1875, but based on earlier depictions of the scene - see Walpole page 101. The second is shown in John Thirtle's "*Thorpe Watering*" - see Allthorpe-Guyton, Plate 42, No. 79.

Continued use of the watering places led to the crumbling away of the road so that both the road and waterings became unsafe. A horse was carried away by the river and drowned. As already mentioned, opposite the waterings was 51 Yarmouth Road. In about 1830, Henry Leathes acquired it, enclosed the land opposite the house and next to Horsewater and began improving it. Leathes and the next owner of No. 51 (H S Patteson) spent at least £100 each raising the road and the riverbank, carting a large quantity of the soil for that purpose and constructing a quay-heading to protect the road (see Eastern Daily Press 16 April 1879).

In 1836, Henry Leathes was granted a license to enclose. The second watering is gone and the area remains enclosed with a boathouse and an area of private moorings. Further east, opposite 53 Yarmouth Road, the green is also enclosed and has been since at least the 1880s. This is presumably for reasons of safety, since the land is narrow and steep here.

53 YARMOUTH ROAD

ST ANDREW'S COURT FORMERLY THE RECTORY

On the other side of the road is 53 Yarmouth Road. This was built in the 1860s as a rectory, following the acquisition of the land by the church in December 1863. William Birkbeck granted the church the land and 18 acres of marsh and meadow in exchange for the former rectory (103 Yarmouth Road) and 16 acres of glebe land behind it. The new rectory was built at the same time as the present church (1864-1866). They were planned together. A track that used to run along the western boundary of the old churchyard was incorporated into the grounds of the new rectory. The track was no longer necessary because the new church was built on the site of the buildings the track had previously led to. The house continued in use as the rectory until 1959.

In the 1860s an existing house had been demolished to make way for the rectory. The house can be seen in an early photograph in Supple (opposite page 30). It shows what may be a four bay, three-storey house with a single-storey western extension. Grigor mentions the garden in 1841 when he refers to "several large trees of the cluster pine (*Pinus Pinaster*), in the garden of the Rev W Frost". In 1800 it was referred to as a "Mansion House" and had 5 acres of garden and plantation. It is clear from manor court records that it was built by Robert Baret of Norwich between 1757 and 1773 on the site of a bakery. This may be the "Robert Barett" who was a sheriff of Norwich in 1765.

In 1781 Armstrong described Thorpe as "delightfully situated on a hanging hill", and having "become of late the residence of opulent manufacturers, several of whom have erected extensive buildings in it, and laid out spacious gardens". He continued that the "village of Thorpe is sometimes called the Richmond of Norfolk, and may vie with the proudest and most admired summer retreats in all England."

III: From the Present and Old Churches to Barber Place

THE PRESENT CHURCH

Next to 53 Yarmouth Road (and linked to it by an entry through the boundary wall) is the present parish church of St Andrew (Plate 16). This replaced the old church, the tower of which can be seen in front of it.

According to Supple (pages 108-9), in "May 1862 it was resolved that additional accommodation be provided in the Church, and that no rate be struck, but subscriptions invited. The immediate response was a sum of £520." Two years later, in 1864, it was decided that enlarging the existing, small building was impracticable. To have done so, it would have been necessary to destroy much of the original fabric. Instead, a new church would be built behind the old church, on a site given by William Birkbeck. Work began in the same year.

The reason given for having a new church was to have an "edifice more adapted to the requirements of the increasing population of the village". Between 1801 and 1851 the population of Thorpe Hamlet (the part of Thorpe west of Harvey Lane) had increased rapidly from 74 to 1,811 and so in 1852 a church (St Matthew's) had been built there and the area had become a separate ecclesiastical district. Between 1801 and 1861 the population of the rest of Thorpe (the part of Thorpe east of Harvey Lane) had increased steadily from 335 to 1,072. At the 1851 Religious Census the old church had 267 sittings. The new church was designed to seat "more than 500".

The architect for the new church was Thomas Jeckyll (1827-81). He had been responsible for a number of slightly odd churches, including Holt Methodist Church (1862-3). The present church consists of nave, chancel and south aisle, both the chancel and the aisle ending in an apse. The arrangement was such that, in the words of a Norfolk Chronicle reporter in 1866, "should the building be found too small for the congregation, which its expected improved arrangements will increase, another aisle could be added on the north side without materially interfering with other parts of the structure".

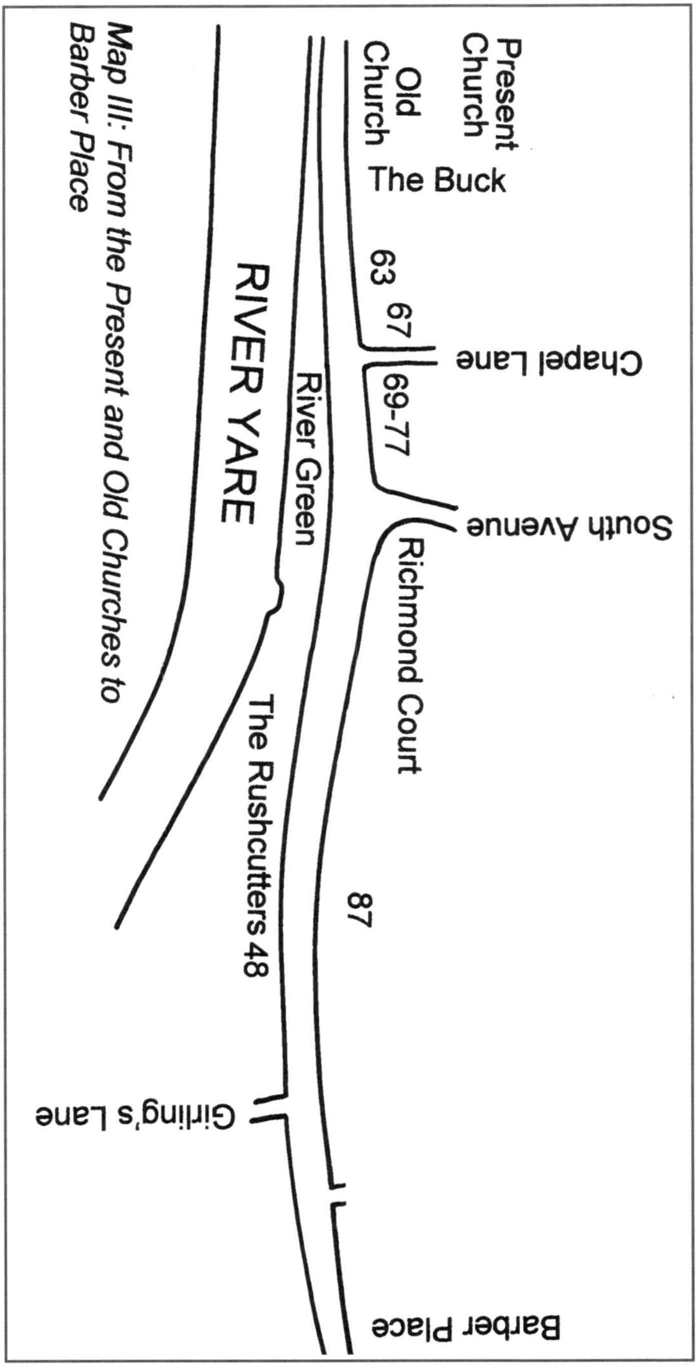

Map III: From the Present and Old Churches to Barber Place

The church is 117 feet (35.5 metres) long and 48 feet (14.5 metres) wide. It is in the "plate tracery" style of the 13th century with elements of Decorated and Transitional. The exterior of the building is of flint, the dressings being of white sandstone, and the roof is of small red square tiles. The reporter referred to above described the outer walls as "exhibiting far too much of that 'station' style of architecture which, in so many instances, at the present day, marks the eccentricities rather than the taste of the designer".

He preferred the interior walls of the new church. They were of warm red brick, relieved by "neat fillets of white brick and squared flint." (The walls are now painted over). The nave is divided from the south aisle by five arches of brick and white stone. The pillars carrying the arches are of red Mansfield marble with Roche Abbey stone capitals.

At the time of the consecration in May 1866, the capitals had been left in their rough state, "the state of the funds not allowing them to be richly carved in foliage as they are designed to be". Stone carving around doorways was left undone. There was also no tower. This was because by 1866 only 75% of the necessary funds (£4,000) had been raised.

The stone carving was probably completed by 1881. Now the most curious feature of the church is the aisle arcade. Pevsner described the "short round piers on high bases with square capitals and abaci, i.e. Transitional, but with colossal capitals, with some semi-Norman motifs but also a pelican and busts of angels."

As well as providing the site, William Birkbeck provided a large proportion of the funds for the new church. Birkbeck was a banker, a shrewd businessman and a benefactor. He was a leading figure in the life of the parish from about 1858 until his death in 1897. He probably saw himself as the successor to John Harvey (see "Thorpe Lodge" above) who was said by the Norwich Mercury in 1866 to "have established the modern prosperity of the village".

An unusual feature of the new church was that, viewed from the road, it was somewhat hidden by the old church. It was intended to let the old church “fall into decay, when a better view of the new will be obtained through the ruins.” It did not decay very quickly.

In 1881 a faculty was obtained “to dilapidate the old church and chancel”. In 1882 the old church was converted into a “picturesque ruin” and a long porch with a tower and spire over it (150 feet or 45.5 metres high) was added to the new church. Bells were added in 1883. In 1944 a landmine explosion cracked the spire. In 1956 a much shorter spire (30 feet or 9 metres high) replaced it.

During the 20th century, changes to the church included a new organ, in 1901, and, in 1920, a chancel screen that was erected as a memorial to the dead of the First World War. The artist, Mr A Kingston Rudd of Sandringham, provided the twelve apostles with portrait heads. In the Eastern Evening News of 14 May 1957, many years after the artist had died, it was disclosed that the portraits were, from left to right: -

St Thomas - Admiral Michael de Ruyter;
St James the Less - from Rubens’ ‘Adoration of the Magi’;
St Bartholomew - Miss Mabel Jacobs;
St Simon - General Sir Dighton Probyn VC;
St John - an American actress (name forgotten by artist);
St Andrew - Bishop King of Lincoln;
St Peter - Lord Salisbury;
St James the Great - Mr Philip Rice of Wolferton;
St Jude - Charles I;
St Matthew - the Rev Henry ffolkes of Hillington;
St Philip - Lord Leighton;
and St Matthias - Bishop King of Lincoln in extreme old age.

THE OLD CHURCH AND THE MOVEMENT OF THE SETTLEMENT

Much of the old church is now in ruins. However, the tower over the south porch remains fully intact. The south and west walls of the nave survive to a substantial extent. The old church was built of coursed flint, brick and limestone. Little remains of the chancel. A spur of masonry shows the line of the chancel south wall. The south respond of the chancel arch is also intact and built of chamfered Tudor brick.

Bryant quotes Mackerell who, writing in 1744, said that the old church was 25 yards (23 metres) long and 7 yards (6 metres) wide and had no aisles (Plate 15). There was a square tower over the south porch with two bells. The tower was no taller than the ridge of the church roof. The nave roof was thatched and the chancel roof tiled. Inside, the altar was raised on two steps and railed in. On the chancel screen were what appear to have been 14th century coats of arms of the Folliot and Hastings families of Elsing,

Plate 15 : The Old Church and part of the Buck, in about 1860.

near East Dereham. There was also an octagonal font of the 15th or 16th century. In addition, there were various memorial stones of the 17th or 18th century, the earliest with a date, according to Mackerell, being 1644. (Norris, writing in the early 1730s, identified a stone dated 1616). Several stones were unidentifiable, having been robbed of their brasses. The most intriguing was an indented stone showing the outline of an armed figure with a lion or dog at his feet and a cushion under his head.

Norris mentioned a “Helmet and two Irons for Pennons” at the east end of the chancel. He speculated that they could have been for Sir Thomas Paston, lord of the manor of Thorpe, who died in 1550. However, he is known to have been buried at Appleton, near King’s Lynn.

In 1815 a small gallery was built at the east end of the nave, approached by a stone staircase in the tower. Schoolchildren used to sit in the gallery.

When the old church was turned into a ruin, many of the monuments from that church were transferred to the long porch of the new church. Having been lost for many years, the font from the old church was discovered and moved into the new church.

The 1864/1866 building of the new church and rectory included changes to the churchyard. Up until then the Buck had been the eastern boundary of the churchyard. The north-west corner of the Buck had marked the line of the churchyard’s northern boundary, which curved slightly southwards to the present curve in the wall immediately south of the access between the present church and 53 Yarmouth Road. Between that boundary and the property to the north, there was a yard that widened towards the east. In the 19th century the yard seems to have contained a cottage and what were probably farm buildings. It was reached by a track that ran between the western boundary of the churchyard and the eastern boundary of the adjoining property.

This yard and track disappeared when space was cleared for the building of the present church and 53 Yarmouth Road (then the new rectory). However, their unusual nature suggests that the church was “planted” on part of an existing plot. This adds weight to the theory that the old church was not Thorpe's original church, but that it was moved to its present site between 1500 and 1550, having previously been located at the top of the Hillside Avenue allotments. (See "The Original Church and Settlement" below).

The theory was first put forward by Rose and Davison in 1988. It means that the old church was built not earlier than the beginning of the 16th century and that any older features it contained (i.e. the font (if it does predate the old church) and the screen) were brought down from the original church. A strong argument for the theory is the liberal use of Tudor brick, for example in the tower. Batcock noted that the tower is constructed of flint but there is a lot of brick. The put-log holes (for scaffolding) are lined with brick. Up to 13 feet (4 metres) from the ground (i.e. about the top of porch level) the quoins are of limestone. Above that, they are of brick. Although this suggests a building break, the use of brick in the arches of the openings above and below the "break" indicates a single phase.

Batcock suggested that the tower resembled a domestic entrance porch of the Tudor period rather than a church tower. He concluded that the tower and the rest of the old church were of one principal phase, and the abundant use of Tudor brick suggested a date in the first half of the 16th century.

Why was the church moved? It is quite likely that this happened in connection with a shift in the focus of settlement from the top of the Hillside Avenue allotments to the river. This may have been linked with a growing importance in river trade and possibly mineral extraction. It may also be linked with the conversion from arable to pasture which seems to have affected the area between Harvey Lane and Thunder Lane in the 15th or 16th century (see "The Original Church and Settlement" below).

Between Thorpe Hall and the Rushcutters, there is direct access to the river from the gravel terrace and so this was an obvious settlement site, although somewhat cramped by the rising ground to the north. The 1600 Mousehold map (Plate 31 in Appendix 2) shows Thorpe Hall and the Rushcutters with the church in a central position along this riverside strip. There are three buildings on either side of the church. The building immediately east of the church may be what is now the Buck. The building east of that may be what is now 63 Yarmouth Road. It has a date-stone of 1586. The Buck and the Rushcutters are likely to date from about 1600.

This suggests a lot of new buildings being erected in the 1580s and 1590s, at least 30 or 40 years after the suggested date for the old church. Also in 1587, some land between the road and the river was given to the church to provide income that could be used towards church repairs (see "Ferryman's Court" above). Repair was needed by 1597, when at the Bishop's visitation, it was reported that the church roof needed thatching, which, in itself, suggests the church must have been built at least 30 or 40 years earlier.

One change that took place between 1461 and 1556 was the building of a new road from Norwich to Thorpe. This included what is now Rosary Road, part of Thorpe Road and Yarmouth Road up to just beyond the railway bridge, where it joined Yarmouth Way. The only part of it that appears to have been completely new was the part between Thunder Lane and the railway bridge. This is because it cut through the existing common field. The rest was probably a development of existing tracks or paths between woodland and meadow or rising ground and the river.

A draft Norwich charter of 1461 describes the eastern boundaries of the city in some detail for the first time. It refers to "a certain way below a wood called Thorpe Wood which leads from Norwich to Postwick above a hill called Leonard's Hill." The reference to "Leonard's Hill" and the way "from Norwich to Postwick" suggests that this was Yarmouth Way. It ran up Gas Hill, then between Mousehold Heath and Thorpe Wood, then eastwards from White Farm Lane to just east of Hilly Plantation, then south-eastwards to just after where the railway bridge crosses Yarmouth Road and then eastwards to Postwick. A new charter of 1556 refers instead "to the high way leading from our said City of Norwich to the vill of Thorpe", which suggests that by this time the new road to Thorpe had been built . Where it joined Yarmouth Way can be seen on the 1585 Mousehold map. It appears to have been a private road belonging to "Mr Gybson". He may be the same person as Thomas Gibson esquire of Thorpe whose will was proved in 1616 and who is the earliest recorded owner of what is now the Rushcutters (see "the Rushcutters" below). The same map shows "the olde churche pathe" leading from the heath, across Yarmouth Way to the original church (see also "the Red Lion" below).

The "moving" of the church, the replanting of the village and the building of a new road suggests the influence of important men. Goreham has suggested the influence of the Pastons, who were lords of the manor of Thorpe from 1547. Although possible, it is unlikely because there is no evidence of them spending money in Thorpe until the late 16th century when Edward Paston rebuilt Thorpe Hall. More likely candidates are the Howards who feature in the history of Thorpe in the 1540s. Their heraldic badge, the White Lion, was the former name of the Buck, the public house immediately to the east of the old church.

In 1542 Henry Howard, Earl of Surrey, obtained a lease of St Leonard's Priory (on the top of Gas Hill), where he began building a great house that became known as Mount Surrey. In 1544 the Howards were granted the lordship of the manor of Thorpe. In 1545 Surrey obtained a lease of St Leonard's Wood. Two years later, in 1547, Surrey was executed for treason.

As far as the old church is concerned, it is very unlikely that Surrey acted on his own. In 1535 the Bishop of Norwich had granted Thomas Godsalve, his Registrar, the patronage of Thorpe church. Godsalve was, according to MacCulloch, "one of a family with close ties to the" Howards. A 1552 inventory of church goods lists simply a bell and "one cope of green say". There is no mention of any communion plate. This may suggest that the church was very poor and had needed to sell most of its goods to raise enough money to comply with new legislation. It is possible that some of the goods had been sold to finance the building of the old church.

One factor that may have been a catalyst for the changes that happened in the 16th century was the forced departure, in 1536, of the Bishop of Norwich as the lord of the manor and principal landowner. The lands were seized by Henry VIII, who held them until 1544. This release from episcopal control may have created the right conditions for the changes.

RIVER GREEN AND ITS MANY USES
(INCLUDING AS THE SITE OF THE FIRST POORHOUSE)

On the other side of the road is River Green (Plate 16).

As mentioned already, the green was a watering place for horses and cattle (see "Horsewater and the Watering Place" above). Until about 1800, it stretched unenclosed from Horsewater to what was the edge of Thorpe Gardens (now the wall of the public toilets near what is now the Rushcutters). As well as a watering place, the green was also a common staithe, where goods could be loaded and unloaded from vessels.

In 1757, the owners of the houses facing the green claimed this right. They said that for a great length of time they had unloaded and loaded keels and lighters there and had erected a staithe. At that time the loads would have included large quantities of marl and lime chalk that had been dug from the Thorpe pits. For example, it is clear from 18th century manor court rolls that the tenants of the Buck had rights over the 25 yards (23 metres) of common staithe opposite their premises. The tenants of the limekiln immediately north of the Buck also had rights over this part of the staithe and this included rights to "leave and lay" on the staithe "stones, gravel, lime, sand and chalk" from the kiln.

It is clear from material in the Rye Manuscripts that by 1766 rights over the green extended to all copyhold tenants of the manor. A tenant claimed they had the right to dig pits and fell top wood. This was not challenged. By 1766 the parish, which owned the land where the parish staithe now is, were claiming rights over the green. This is why, at about that time, they erected a parish staithe and enclosed it with iron railings. It may have been on the same site as the staithe that was erected in 1844 at the end of the green between where the present public staithe is (opposite the Hearts Cruisers' office that is on the other side of the river) and the wall of the toilet block. The intention may have been that this staithe should supersede the common staithe rights. It continued in use during the 19th century.

From an unknown date until 1769, the village poorhouse (or town house) "stood by the riverside" between "the Road and the Common River about

100 yards (91 metres) from the Church". This suggests it stood on the green opposite Chapel Lane, not far from where the war memorial now stands. However, it may have been on the site of what is now the public staithe, since this was land that belonged to the parish. The town house was described as a cottage that was divided into three tenements.

In 1776 village stocks were acquired from Postwick and set up on the green opposite the church. They are depicted in James Stark's "*View on the Yare, near Thorpe Church*", published in 1829. According to Supple (page 95), the stocks were there until 1852.

The 1841 tithe map shows a parish lock-up, known as "The Cage", standing by the riverside on what is now the public staithe, opposite what is now Richmond Court. Before a regular police force began in 1840s, the parish constable was responsible for the village stocks and lock-up. A lock-up was a gaol where felons were detained pending their removal to court and drunks and troublemakers were locked up for the night. Supple (page 95) quotes someone who remembered it as "a sort of box" that "was erected to save taking a prisoner up to Norwich at a late hour." He believed "only one prisoner was ever put in it – probably for drunkenness – and when he awoke next morning, not knowing where on earth he was, he nearly, as they say, 'went off his head'. "

Thirtle's *Thorpe St Andrew* (see Allthorpe-Guyton Plate 40 No. 80) and John Crome's *View on the Yare* (see Clifford, Plate 121a) show a small building by the riverside towards the Rushcutters. It is not clear what this was. (It has been suggested that it was where the water-cart was kept that was used for laying dust on the road).Vestry minutes show that the lock-up referred to above was not erected until 1834. By the 1880s it had gone and a group of trees had been planted in its place. The Ordnance Survey 25 inch map of the 1880s shows a pump on the edge of the green opposite the south-eastern corner of the churchyard.

There were several attempts in the 19th century to enclose a part of the green. They failed. The third attempt, in 1879, was described as "an attempt at depriving the parish of a very valuable source of recreation to them, as also it was to that numerous section of the Norwich public that found its summer pleasure for the most part on the river."

In 1855 the parishioners put down posts and rails to protect the green. In 1919 the lord of the manor gave the green to the parish council and a war memorial was erected there.

THE BUCK

FORMERLY THE WHITE LION

On the north side of the road, next to the church, is the Buck (Plate 16). This is a brick and flint building that descends in stages of height towards the road. There are four sections. The section furthest from the road is probably 17th century and has lucarne windows. The section adjoining this (now pierced by a modern porch) may be 18th century. The two sections nearest the road are probably 19th century, but may have been partly rebuilt. They contain flint particularly on the churchyard side. These two latter sections may have originated as outbuildings. A photograph of about 1880 shows that at that time there was no chimney and so these sections were unheated. The tenant of the Buck in the late 1870s was also a coal merchant. He advertised this with a sign on the gable end of the higher of these two sections "COALS SOLD HERE". This suggests they were used in connection with his coal business. A coal business may also have been run from here in the 1840s and 1850s. The tenant at that time was referred to in 1850 as a "coal dealer".

Before about 1775 the Buck was known as the White Lion. It is clear from 18th century manor court rolls, that, below the north end of the building, there was a cellar. There was also a gate or gateway across a passage separating the Buck and its yard from the limekiln that lay to the north. From the churchyard wall to the eastern side of the yard of the Buck was 23 yards (21 metres). The owners of the limekiln had the right to transport materials through the yard to the road. They could leave and lay them on the 25 yards (23 metres) of staithe near the river over which the Buck had rights. The yard of the Buck comprised a walled enclosure east of the two lower sections of the building and a passageway that ran between the Buck and this enclosure. The wall around the enclosure was demolished in the 1920s, when a garage and stable were built there. The yard is now used as a car park.

In the 19th century the eastern half of the present car park was part of the neighbouring property – 63 Yarmouth Road. It was occupied by two buildings (Plate 16). Immediately west of and adjoining No. 63 was a building

Plate 16 : View across the river and the green to 53 Yarmouth Road, the Present and Old Churches, the Buck and the buildings immediately west of 63 Yarmouth Road, in about 1905.

that was there by 1881, was a post office in 1901 and several years later was a cycle shop. West of that was a building set back from the road. It was there by 1841 and occupied by a shoe maker. From at least 1850 to the 1870s, it was a post office. In about 1905 this small building was demolished and a bigger taller "Tudor-style" building with half-timbering was erected on the roadside (back cover). Both buildings were demolished in about 1960.

The track that ran along the eastern side of the Buck seems to have continued northwards as far as the Chapel Lane / South Avenue pit. In fact, before the pit blocked it, it may have continued northwards to Yarmouth Way.

63 YARMOUTH ROAD

FORMERLY THE HOMESTEAD

Before 1786, the property consisted of three-quarters of an acre of land and included a barn and other buildings on the site of what is now 67 Yarmouth Road. In 1786 what is now 67 Yarmouth Road was sold off.

In 1800 the property was described as "a Dwelling-House, Stable, and Cart, Chaise or Coach House, Two Cottages and about a quarter of an acre of land." The cottages were probably those that can be seen on the 1841 tithe map on the northern boundary of the site, by a pathway that led to Chapel Lane, along the southern boundary of what is now 8A Chapel Lane. As already mentioned (see "The Buck" above), in about 1841 and 1881 cottages were erected by the roadside west of the house. Also, in 1883, "Church Cottages" were built north-west of the house, divorcing it from its garden.

In 1993 Edwin Rose carried out an archaeological survey of the building. The basic structure consists of a line of four rooms. The earlier rooms are the rooms on either side of the central axial stack. The rooms at the north and south ends are later additions. It seems that the building began, probably in the late 16th century, as a small brick and flint building, now represented by the room south of the central stack. A datestone of 1586 may relate to this, although it is not in its original position. In the early 17th century, a grand three-storey, timber-framed parlour block was added, to the north of the original building. It included a new or remodelled stack. It had a single storey extension to the north and possibly a cellar. The rooms at the north and south ends of the present building were added, probably in the 19th century, the south wall being rebuilt in 1880 by its then owner John Henry Piggott. The date-stone reads "JHP 1880".

It appears from the 1841 tithe map that at that time the house was divided into three dwellings. There may have been a shop or workshop in the middle section, because the occupier was described as "a grocer and a silversmith". In the 1871 census the building is referred to as "Dial House". By 1891 it was known as "The Homestead".

67 YARMOUTH ROAD

IDLE HOUR

In 1800 the building that stood on this site was described as "cottages". By the 1880s it is clear that it was divided into three, the largest unit being towards the north. The building extended southwards as far as the street and faced out to Chapel Lane. At the time of the 1861 census, part of the building was occupied by a "General Shopkeeper", who in 1871 was referred to as a baker and grocer. By 1881 it was a post office. By 1891, the post office had moved and the building was referred to as "Old Post Office Yard".

In the late 1890s, the cottages were pulled down, the western boundary was moved towards No. 63 and Idle Hour was built. Unlike the cottages, it was set back from the street. It was also wider than the cottages had been. In about 1920 the gable end at the front of the building was extended slightly and a northern extension was added.

An 1893 photograph of the southern end of the cottages shows that they were of flint with stone quoins. When the new house was built, the cottages were not demolished completely. Part of the eastern wall of the cottages and, probably, the cellars, were incorporated. This part of the eastern wall is irregular in construction and includes flint and brick. A manor court entry of 1786 suggests that some or all of the cottages had been part of a barn. Much of the fabric of the barn seems to have been retained when the conversion into cottages occurred in the 1790s. Some of it can be seen in the east wall of Idle Hour today.

CHAPEL LANE

Chapel Lane may have originated as an access way to a chalk pit. A manor court entry of 1786 refers to it as "the way leading to the lime kiln in the use of William Brinded." At the northern end of the lane, there appears to have been a quarry, with a later large pit dug into it on the eastern side. Before the Second World War, the pit used to come through as far as South Avenue. After the war, this part of the pit was filled in. It has now been built over.

Chapel Lane was named after a Congregationalist chapel that was built there in 1839 (Plate 17). Revd. John Alexander, pastor of Princes Street Congregationalist Church, began the Thorpe Mission in 1829. The chapel that was built ten years later was also used as a day school. It had seats for 150. On Sundays there were afternoon and evening services. In 1851 there was an average congregation of 60 at each service. This compared with 105 at the church. The average Sunday school attendance at the chapel was 40 on a Sunday afternoon, compared with a combined morning and afternoon total of 93 at the church . In 1897 the chapel closed and was purchased by the church as a mission room and parish hall. It was demolished in the late 1980s. The site is now occupied by 8A to 8D Chapel Lane.

Plate 17 : Parish hall (formerly a Congregationalist chapel), Chapel Lane, in 1987.

Opposite them are 12 and 14 Chapel Lane. At the time of the 1901 census, the building they occupy was a working-men's club. By the 1930s, it had been converted into two houses.

Probably the oldest buildings in the lane are the cottages north of 12 and 14 Chapel Lane. Their date-stone reads "KH 1820." "KH" was Roger Kerrison Harvey, John Harvey's third son. He is named as the owner of the cottages in the 1841 tithe records.

At that time, he also owned the row of flint and brick cottages that run off westwards at the end of Chapel Lane. By 1881 there were 11 of them, although the 1891 census only refers to 10. In that census, the row is referred to as "Rotten Row" – "rotten" suggesting soft yielding ground, possibly a reference to the quarry to the north, east and west.

The name Chapel Lane first appears in the 1851 census. Censuses from 1851 to 1881 also refer to all or part of the lane as "Green Hills".

69, 73, 75 AND 77 YARMOUTH ROAD

Nos. 69 and 73 (Plate 18) are flint and brick cottages with single storey extensions at the front. They were there in 1825 and probably in 1800. In 1841 No. 69 was a shoemakers and No.73 a bakery. No. 73 is now Chris Denham – newsagent and general stores.

No. 75 is an end-on house that dates from at least 1825. In 1841 it was divided into three cottages. In 1891 the first one was the post office and the other two were called "Post Office Yard".

No. 77 is a 19th century house extended to the street in 1902, when Walter Parker built on a shop and lounge with a roof garden and bedroom above. This was the post office and general stores that Walter's sisters, brother and then nephew ran until the late 1950s. It is now Harleys.

Between 1800 and 1825, what is now South Avenue - and was then a track - was diverted slightly westwards to give "Dunollie" (see "Richmond Court" below) a bigger garden. One result was the demolition of a row of cottages west of No. 77 that had faced the track.

Plate 18 : 69, 73, 75 and 77 Yarmouth Road and Dunollie (now Richmond Court), in about 1905.

SOUTH AVENUE
(INCLUDING THE SITE OF THOMPSON'S FOLLY)

South Avenue probably originated as a north-south track continuing northwards to Yarmouth Way, meeting it just south of the ends of the back gardens on the southern side of Hill Crest Road. However, it may be that, since medieval times, it has led to the farm that used to be immediately north of High House (see "The Original Church and Settlement" below).

On a hill in Weston Wood, near the end of Western Avenue, there used to be a tower (Plate 19). In 1800 it was referred to as "Thompson's Folly" which suggests it was built in the 1760s or 1770s by Nockold Thompson, who owned nearby land. By 1783, it appears to have belonged to the rector, Richard Humfrey. In that year, Sylas Neville wrote in his diary:-

"The parsonage commands the river & meadows with the road to Yarmouth, but from the grove behind, which is on a bank, there are a variety of delightful views.... there are none better than those from Mr Humphrey's Belvidere.... The river barges under sail, rich meadows and woods, country seats with mills etc. in picturesque situations."

Plate 19 : The tower in Weston Wood ("Thompson's Folly") in the 1950s.

Faden's map of Norfolk, surveyed in the early 1790s, refers to the tower as "Thorpe Gazebo" and shows a circle of trees around it. Grigor, in 1841, refers to it as "a lonely watch-tower ... almost clad with ivy". Part of the tower was still standing in the 1950s and is depicted in a small drawing in the Eastern Evening News of 13 August 1955. The tower was of flint and was said to have "three rooms, one on top of another". It is no longer visible.

By 1813 what is now South Avenue had become the private road to a newly-built house called "the Grove" (later rebuilt as "High House") and the farm that adjoined it to the north. In about 1910 "lodges" were built, one near the bottom of South Avenue and the other, "North Lodge" (93 Thunder Lane), on the line of Yarmouth Way, nearly opposite Hilly Plantation.

Between South Avenue and Stanmore Road, there is evidence of a pit. In 1841 this was referred to as "the Dell".

RICHMOND COURT

THE SITE OF DUNOLLIE

These flats were built in the 1930s on the site of a large house that had been known from at least 1891 as "Dunollie" (Plate 18). As mentioned above, between 1800 and 1825, South Avenue was diverted slightly westwards to give the house a bigger garden (see " 69, 73, 75 and 77 Yarmouth Road" above). This increased its grounds from 0.88 acres to 1.07 acres.

18th century copyhold deeds refer to a cartway (now South Avenue) on the western edge of the property and "an ancient footway now disused" on the northern boundary. The latter may have been a path between the house plots and the closes that lay to the north of them that are shown on the 1600 Mousehold map (Plate 31 in Appendix 2). Changes in boundaries and redevelopment of the site make the line of the path difficult to follow now. It is likely that part of it ran along what was the northern boundary of 63 Yarmouth Road. This equates with the southern boundary of 8A Chapel Lane. No right of way exists today.

THE RUSHCUTTERS
FORMERLY THE BOAT AND BOTTLE, PREVIOUSLY THORPE GARDENS, ORIGINALLY THE TUNS

On the other side of the road is the Rushcutters.

According to Stephen Heywood's 1998 survey, the building dates from about 1600. Its first-recorded owner, Thomas Gibson esquire of Thorpe, may have built it. His will was proved in 1616 (see also "The Old Church and the Movement of the Settlement" above).

Heywood identified a six-bay timber frame, with an original brick and flint east gable end, including an original stack. The two easternmost bays were the parlour and parlour chambers. The hall was probably in the two bays further west. The two westernmost bays may have contained the service rooms. The large western stack was probably added during the 17th century. In the middle of the 19th century the west crosswing was added.

Plate 20 : Roadside view of the Tuns (now the Rushcutters) in 1874.

Before 1800 this and the neighbouring property (now 48 Yarmouth Road) were a unit. A deed of 1745 describes them as a "Capital Messuage … and a Great Barn and Malting Office and House with a Cistern of Lead to the said Malting Office and House … and One Garden and Two Orchards and the back Grounds ….. all inclosed with a Stone wall on the west, a Fleet of Water on the east and abutting on the Kings Highway on the north." Attached to the property were 100 acres of "bruery ground" (i.e. heath) called Gargett's Hills (see "The Original Church etc." below) and four acres of meadow. The tenant was John Miller, a malster.

In 1800 what is now 48 Yarmouth Road was sold off. It was described as a "Malthouse" with "a Storehouse and Lean-to adjoining to the west." It was converted into a house. By 1900 it was known as Eastwick and it is now called Monk's Barn. In the 1930s the southern half of the building was demolished, including a wing that abutted the Rushcutters.

In 1800 the Rushcutters was described in a deed as a "Capital Messuage now used as Public house and called … the Tuns … with Barns, Stables, Houses …Gardens, Bowling-Green." The tenant was Robert Cattermoul. Adjoining the buildings were two cottages. A Norwich directory of 1783 refers to a freemasons' lodge that met at the Tuns in Thorpe and had been founded in 1766. It therefore appears to have been a public house since at least that date.

By 1825 the tenant was Thomas William Hinsby. James Stark's "*Hinsby's Gardens, Thorpe*" was published in 1829. This shows a very truncated view of the building, but it does illustrate that by this time the western half of the site had been laid out as a lawn with covered arbours or boxes on the north and east sides, that looked like cloisters.

In 1843 the present western crosswing was added. In September of that year there is a newspaper reference to Mr Cattermole's "splendid new room", which was the large club room on the first floor of the new wing. The eastern "cloister" of the lawn was incorporated within the ground floor of the new building. The ground floor was also used as skittle alley. The new wing had a sign on the roof - "CATTERMOLE", the name of the new proprietor, Robert Cattermole, probably the son of the tenant who had been there forty years before.

Following John Harvey's death in 1842, Cattermole was a leading light in the Thorpe Regatta and races took place from the Tuns. When this was advertised in the Norwich Mercury of 9 July 1842, the advertisement included an engraving of a rowing boat, a yacht in front and a silver cup in the sky. Superimposed on the picture was a boar under which were the words "Het Varke". This is the sign that from about the 1850s until 1969 hung over the back door of the public house facing the river (Plate 21). It was a blue pig with golden tusks, with the words "Het Varke" inscribed beneath. "Het Varke" is Dutch for "this pig". It was suggested by Hooper (Eastern Daily Press 19 November 1895) that it was a "relic probably of some ill-fated Batvian coaster, lost or broken on East Anglian shores." There is better explanation.

Thomas Vere was lord of the manor of Thorpe from 1751 until 1766. His family crest matches the sign, because it is described as "a boar passant

Plate 21 : Riverside view of Thorpe Gardens (now the Rushcutters) in about 1905, with, on the right, the "Het Varke" sign.

azure attired or". There is no evidence that the Veres ever owned the building or lived there. The earliest photograph of the Tuns, taken in about 1845, does not show the sign. It appears first on a slightly later photograph, probably taken in the 1850s. The Vere school was closed in 1841 (see "Ferryman's Court" above). Cattermole may have acquired the sign from there.

By 1883 the name of the inn had changed to Thorpe Gardens. A plan of 1888 shows the site was split into two areas. In the western half were the gardens with a lawn in middle and terraces and seats (some sheltered) around it. In the eastern half was the public house facing the river with seats in front of it. By the date of the plan, the skittle alley had become a boathouse. Behind the public house was a yard, with stables and a kitchen garden and access from the road.

By the 1920s (i.e. between 1912 and 1926) the "cloister" on the northern side of lawn had been demolished. During the 1930s the short eastern extension to the main block, that may have once been a cottage, also went. In 1956, as part of road widening, the northern boundary of the lawn area was moved further south. In 1969 the name of the public house was changed to the Boat and Bottle and, in 1985, it changed again to the Rushcutters.

87 YARMOUTH ROAD

On the opposite side of the road to the Rushcutters is 87 Yarmouth Road. This large late 18th century house has a pilastered classical south door. Jehoshaphat Postle, a beer brewer, and then his son (of the same name) owned the Rushcutters (then the Tuns) from 1754 until 1800. It is likely that they built and lived at 87 Yarmouth Road. In 1841 Sarah Postle, the second Jehoshaphat's daughter-in-law, was living there with two daughters and five servants. Of the houses along Yarmouth Road in 1841, this number of servants was only exceeded by John Harvey at Thorpe Lodge who had ten and Charles Weston at Thorpe House who had six.

In the 20th century the house was known as "the Dell". In 1956 the stables and part of the south wing were reduced in size, when the road was widened.

GIRLING'S LANE
(INCLUDING THE SITE OF THE RAILWAY ACCIDENT)

On the other side of the road is Girling's Lane. Near the end of the lane is a railway crossing. The Yarmouth and Norwich Railway was opened on April 30th 1844, work having begun on the track a year earlier. To accommodate the railway, bridges were built across the river south of Thorpe Hall and south of the Rushcutters. To avoid having two opening bridges within a mile, a channel was excavated from Trowse Hythe to Whitlingham Reach, known as the New Cut. The main river traffic now used this route.

Just before the railway crossing on Girling's Lane, there is a commemorative stone, recording the terrible railway accident that occurred here on September 10th 1874. An express train from Norwich collided with a mail train from Brundall. The drivers and the firemen of both locomotives were killed, eighteen passengers were killed on the spot, and about fifty were severely wounded, of whom five died during the next few days. The dead and the dying were taken to the Tuns (now the Rushcutters), and the injured to the Norfolk and Norwich Hospital.

Girling's Lane is named after the boat hirers and builders who, in the 1920s and 1930s, had a boatyard on the far side of the railway line.

IV: From 103 Yarmouth Road to School Avenue

103 YARMOUTH ROAD

THE OLD RECTORY

On the other side of the road is 103 Yarmouth Road. Although there have been alterations, this is basically the rectory that was built in 1754. It is of brick and has 5 bays and 3 storeys.

A memorandum in the parish register by Richard Humfrey, rector of Thorpe from 1753 until 1813, reads:-

"1754 - The Parsonage House, having been entirely taken down and rebuilt, was finished this Year and the Wash-house rebuilt, the Barn new thatched with reed, the South End of the Stable built, the Hay Chamber Floor, the Partitions, Rack, Manger, etc. were all put up new and the stable paved, large new doors made to the Hay-house and the whole put in good repair. The Garden on the South side of the House was also made this year... wall next to the Road built and the Gates... put up all new."

A glebe terrier of 1763 refers to the house as having "two parlours, hall, study, kitchen with chamber and garrets over". It also refers to "two barns, a stable and other outhouses".

Entries in the rector's accounts include:-
Sept 12 1754 "Paid for Stone to put up at East end of House with the Date when it was built 6s".
Nov 16 1754 "Paid for a Roof-raising Treat to the Workmen that built the new Parsonage £1 9s 9d".

A 1692 terrier includes a description of the previous rectory. It contained "one Kitchen, one Buttery or Pantry with an entry on the south side, one Hall, one Parlour with Chambers of a second storey over each and a third storey except over the Hall." This suggests a timber-framed (?) house with a hall open to the roof in the middle, service rooms (with rooms over them) and an entry at one end and a parlour (with rooms over it) at the other end.

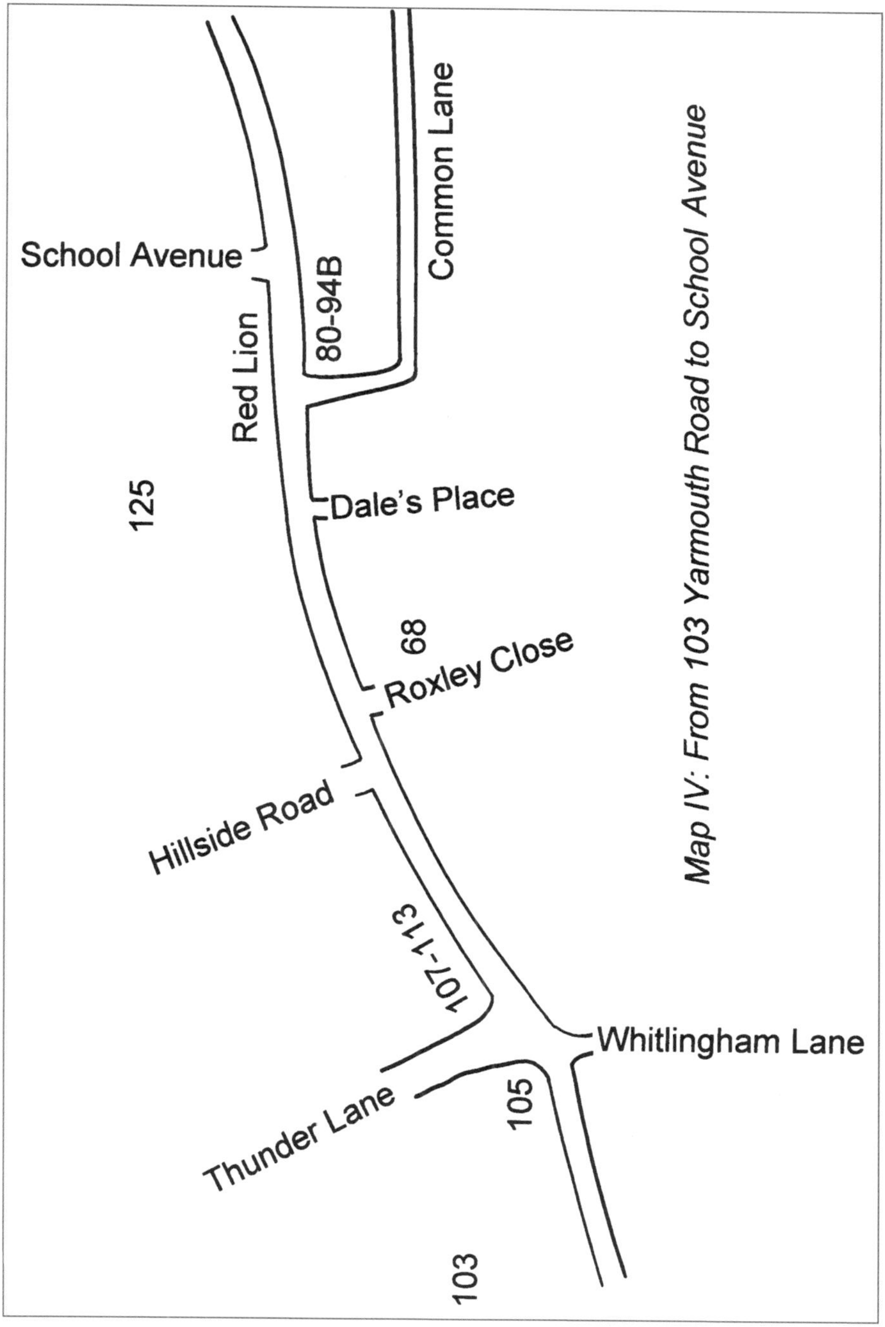

Map IV: From 103 Yarmouth Road to School Avenue

From descriptions of 1692 and 1699, it appears there was a large stone barn 90 feet (27.5 metres) in length and 20 feet (6 metres) in breadth. There was a timber-framed hay-house at the north end and a "lading" at the south end. On the west side was a timber-framed dairy. There was also a smaller barn of 27 feet (8 metres) by 21 feet (6.5 metres) with a stable and pigsties and a cattle-shed with a hay chamber over them at the south end and a cart house at the end of them.

As mentioned under "53 Yarmouth Road" above, in 1863 the rectory changed hands as part an exchange of land between William Birkbeck and the church. In 1872 Birkbeck sold it to Charlotte Herring, widow of Armine Herring, rector of Thorpe from 1857 until 1867.

East of the former rectory is a former coach-house that, from map evidence, was built between 1841 and the 1880s.

105 YARMOUTH ROAD
FORMERLY THE WHITE HOUSE

Although it has been altered, the present house is basically a late 18th century house, with a shaped gable and blocked windows at the rear, that appear to be remnants of a 17th century house. It seems from maps of 1825 and 1841 that the 18th century house was built as a southern extension of the17th century house. By the 1880s there had been numerous changes to the house. They may have obliterated much of the 17th century building. A modern brick extension has been attached to the east front of the building.

A clue to the early development of the house comes with its link to the Johnson charity. William Johnson, an apothecary from Arminghall, owned the property in about 1700. He wanted to extend his garden eastwards and so take in some of Thunder Lane. This he did and it explains the kink that used to be in Thunder Lane at the junction with Yarmouth Road. (The kink

Plate 22 : Albert Place (formerly Tan Yard) in 1953 (now 1 Thunder Lane and an access to 103 Yarmouth Road).

was removed when, in 1959, the road was widened and an old oak tree removed). It was agreed that in compensation for taking in some of the roadway, he should pay the churchwardens and overseers of the parish £1 a year. When he died in 1705, aged 74, the money became a rentcharge on his house. According to an 1839 Charity Commissioners report, the money was used at Christmas to buy "threepenny loaves" for the "poorest persons of the parish". In a survey of between 1700 and 1731 there is a reference to "Johnson" at "Halfway house". This may be an earlier name for the house.

A manor court roll of 1785 refers to the house as being "formerly Yallops". According to an inscription in the church, Robert Yallop "died at his house in this town 28 July 1656 aged 55". He was buried in the old church. He was the father of Sir Robert who acquired the manor of Bowthorpe in 1660, was knighted in 1664 and died in 1705 aged 68. Sir Robert was a strong Catholic. If Robert was also a Catholic, he would have not been alone in Thorpe in the 17th century. Edward Paston and his grandson Clement were leading Catholics, as was Robert Blofeld, rector of Thorpe from 1642 until 1670.

In 1800 the house was described as a "farmhouse" that had "several barns outhouses and other buildings and 216 acres of land". It was owned and occupied by Isaac Marsh. From the 1860s the house was known as Covey House. It was later called the White House.

By 1830 the buildings immediately north of the house (now 1 Thunder Lane and an access way to 103 Yarmouth Road) were being used as a tannery. In 1860s what in 1841 had been Golding Allen's "Tan Office and premises" had become a yard with cottages on the north and east sides and the outbuildings of the then rectory on the west side. By 1891 there were 14 cottages in "Tan Yard", which was also known as Albert Place (Plate 22). Two of them had only two rooms, three had three rooms and the others had four rooms.

WHITLINGHAM LANE

On the other side of the road is Whitlingham Lane. This is so-called because, until the 1840s, you could walk along the lane, crossing the meadow, continue south along a riverside path until the eastward bend in the river and then cross the river by ferry to Whitlingham. In 1845, the ferry was run by Ann King, keeper of the White House tavern in Trowse, close to the Whitlingham parish boundary.

White's Norfolk of 1845 describes Whitlingham:-
"The church (St Andrew) was dilapidated about 1630, and now forms a picturesque ruin, near the verge of a lofty precipice, overlooking the river. The tavern called Whitlingham White House is in Trowse Newton parish, and has a ferry across the Yare. Pleasure parties often visit this spot to enjoy its romantic scenery and remarkable echo."

In 1869 Bayne wrote in his History of Norwich:-
"The road from the Foundry bridge to Thorpe village is a favourite walk of the citizens [of Norwich]. .... On the south side of the river, which was once reached by the ferry boat, stands the village of Whitlingham, where the citizens formerly resorted by thousands in the summer months. The grounds in this locality present a pleasing variety of hill and dale, wood and water, and the view from the White House includes the windings of the 'bonny Yare,' the opposite village of Thorpe, [and, in Norwich,] the spire of the Cathedral and the frowning aspect of the old Norman Castle".

The White House tavern appears to have been demolished in about 1860 and rebuilt as a thatched cottage (also called the White House) a few years later. The 12th century round tower of Whitlingham church collapsed in 1940.

According to Robinson and Rose, Thunder Lane is part of a Roman road between Brampton and Thorpe. There may have been a Romano-British riverside settlement at Thorpe. Whitlingham Lane and the ferry-crossing appear to be a continuation of Thunder Lane. This suggests that Whitlingham Lane, and possibly the ferry crossing, are of similar age to Thunder Lane.

In 1844 the railway line crossed Whitlingham Lane. Whitlingham Station was opened in 1874, as part of the development of the adjacent Whitlingham junction from which a new line branched off to North Walsham. (This was extended, three years later, to Cromer). Whitlingham Station closed to passenger services in 1955 and general goods in 1964. It stood immediately east of the footbridge that was erected over the line in 1886.

THUNDER LANE

On the other side of the road to Whitlingham Lane is Thunder Lane. It may have originated as a Roman road (see "Whitlingham Lane" above). Its continued importance during the medieval period and up to 1801 was as a drove way for taking cattle and sheep to and from Mousehold Heath. On the 1585 Mousehold map, it is called Drovegate. Until 1801, Thunder Lane crossed Yarmouth Way just south of Hilly Plantation and entered Mousehold Heath just south of Laundry Close. Thunder Lane probably continued as a track across the heath. When Mousehold was turned into fields in 1801, the track was straightened and made into a road.

Thunder Lane is probably named after the Thunder family who owned property in Thorpe in the late 15th and early 16th centuries. The will of John Thundir of Thorpe was proved in 1500.

Yarmouth Way can still be seen as a hollow way running through the front gardens of 17, 18 and 19 Hilly Plantation. To the east are allotments that are accessible from Hillside Avenue. If you imagine the hollow way running through the northern end of the allotments, it would pass the site of the first church of Thorpe St Andrew.

THE ORIGINAL CHURCH AND SETTLEMENT

In May 1951 Mr D.W. Aldous was planting potatoes in a newly cleared allotment just east of Hilly Plantation. He noticed some masonry and bone fragments but assumed they were from muck spreading. Then his dog found a human jaw. He had discovered a church that had been forgotten for at least 300 years. Rose and Davison subsequently identified this as the first church of Thorpe St Andrew.

A. P. Baggs, R. R. Clarke and A. J. Martin excavated the site at intervals from 1951 until 1953 (Plate 23). The earliest evidence was of late Saxon

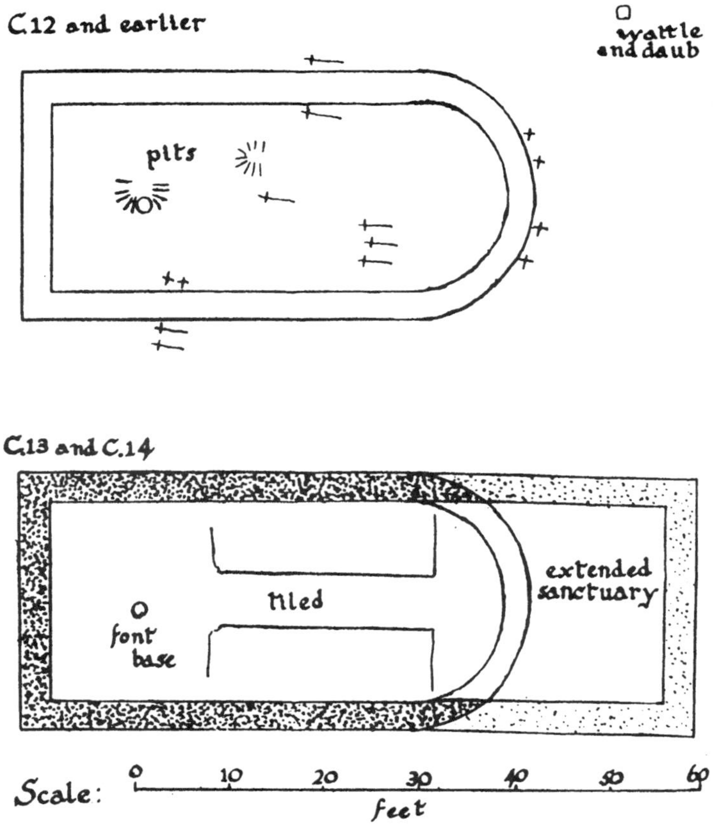

Plate 23 : Plans of the original church, drawn following the 1951-53 excavations.

domestic occupation, with refuse pits containing pottery, loom-weights and a decorated silver pinhead of Viking type. In the 11th century the site had been used as a burial ground. Some of the burials were then disturbed, probably in the early 12th century, by the construction of a single-celled, apsidal-ended church that was 55 feet (17 metres) by 25 feet (7.5 metres), including walls 3 feet (1 metre) thick and possibly red floor tiles. Probably in the early 13th century, a rectangular chancel with poor foundations was added to the church, extending the total length of the building to 70 feet (21.5 metres). By the 14th century the nave floor was covered with tiles with yellow, red and green glaze and a font had been added at the west end. The chancel screen (described in "The Old Church etc." above) had been built.

The late Saxon domestic occupation is important evidence of post-Roman occupation of Thorpe. As well as the pits, a wattle and daub building was found that was either late Saxon or early Norman. In Thorpe, late Saxon pottery has also been discovered just north of 16 Harvey Lane (The Oaks), which is also not far south of Yarmouth Way. Late Saxon (as well as 13th/14th century) pottery has also been found near where the path from Whitlingham Lane first reaches the river i.e. after the dyke. This suggests perhaps a place where goods were loaded and unloaded.

It is tempting to link the 11th century burial ground with Stigand. He is the first-recorded lord of the manor of Thorpe. He was Bishop of East Anglia from 1042 and was probably granted Thorpe by Edward the Confessor at that time, although he may have received it earlier since he had been an influential royal adviser from at least 1020.

In 1101 Henry I granted the manor of Thorpe to Bishop Herbert. The Bishops of Norwich had a manor house at Thorpe, at least from the first half of the 13th century. Herbert was a great church-builder e.g. Norwich Cathedral and the priory churches of St Nicholas, Great Yarmouth and St Margaret, Kings Lynn. It is highly likely that he built the original church. It may have been the last in a series of churches he built along the edge of Thorpe Wood / Mousehold Heath. It would have followed on from Magdalen Chapel (now the Lazar House library, Sprowston Road), St. Michael's Chapel and St Leonard's Priory.

The original church was immediately south of Yarmouth Way and east of what is now 19 Hilly Plantation. After passing the church, Yarmouth Way turned east-south-eastwards and ran down towards where the railway bridge now crosses Yarmouth Road. It then turned eastwards to the boundary with Postwick.

Thorpe's first church was a roadside church, about 170 yards (155 metres) south of Mousehold Heath. Its position suggests that the village of Thorpe grew up along Yarmouth Way – perhaps between near where Yarmouth Way crossed Thunder Lane at "North Lodge" (93 Thunder Lane) and where it crossed what is now Pound Lane. Faden's map of Norfolk, surveyed in the early 1790s, shows a rectangular enclosure in the vicinity of Lodge Place and High House, near where Yarmouth Way crossed Thunder Lane. It is also marked on the 1700 / 1731 sketch maps. This seems to be the site of a farm that was there before Mousehold was enclosed in 1801. (It is also a possible candidate for the pre-13th or pre-14th century manor house site (see "Thorpe Hall - Description and early history" above). The 1585 Mousehold map shows that the land west of Thunder Lane and between Yarmouth Way and Mousehold Heath was demesne land i.e. it belonged to the lord of the manor. This may increase the possibility that the manor house site was nearby).

Between the original church and what is now Pound Lane, Yarmouth Way ran down east-south-eastwards along what are now the northern boundaries of the allotments and Hillside Avenue County Primary School. It then continued in the same direction between Highfield Close and St Andrew's Close, crossing Pound Lane immediately south of the Sainsbury's site. North of this part of Yarmouth Way was an area of Mousehold Heath of about 100 acres known as Gargytt Hills (the 1585 Mousehold map), Gargett Hills (the 1600 Mousehold map), Gargett's Hills (a 1745 title deed for the Rushcutters) or Gargate holes, hole or hill (the 1841 tithe map). If the correct form is Gargate, it may be an alternative name for Yarmouth Way, the prefix "gar" being linked with earlier forms of the name of the River Yare. It is also possible that it was a name that was associated with the settlement that grew up along this part of Yarmouth Way. (An area of woodland north of the Ring Road that in 1841 was called Gargate hill plantation has since at least the 1880s been called "Garglehill Plantation").

Thorpe is depicted on the 1600 Mousehold map (Plate 31 in Appendix 2). The part of Thorpe east of Thunder Lane seems to have a different character from the rest of the parish. It is only in this part of Thorpe that you find an open field, the low riverside common and, across the river, the parish of Whitlingham. This may, in part, be because of changes to the landscape west of Thunder Lane. Field boundaries on the 1841 tithe map suggest that, before these changes, between Thunder Lane and what is now Dale's Loke / Bishop's Close (or, more precisely, a north/south line east of the building that is now 51 Yarmouth Road), there was an open field. Between Dale's Loke / Bishop's Close and Harvey Lane, there were irregular fields, probably taken in from Thorpe Wood in the 13th or 14th century (see "Thorpe Hall - Description and early history" above). By the time of the 1600 Mousehold map, the whole area had been converted largely to pasture, either enclosed or left open to Mousehold. This change probably happened in the 15th or 16th century, when pasture land became profitable through the growth in demand for wool.

There may once have been a link between the churches of Thorpe and Whitlingham. Both churches are dedicated to St Andrew, as are Trowse to the west of Whitlingham and Kirby Bedon to the south. Whitlingham church is situated on a hill and is mentioned in Domesday. It may have been Thorpe's "mother-church".

The church at Thorpe lacked aisles or a tower. This suggests a poor community who could not afford to add to their church. It may also suggest a small community that did not need a larger church for a growing population. The principal change to the church was the extension and squaring of the chancel in the early 13th century. This was the date ascribed to the masonry mass found at the time of the excavation. Since the chancel was the responsibility of the rector or patron (the Bishop of Norwich), he rather than the parish, would have been responsible for extending it, probably to provide more liturgical space.

Although the bishop had a major house in the parish, there is no suggestion that, (apart from appointing priests), he had a major involvement in the church. For reasons mentioned under "Thorpe Hall - Description and early history" above, it is likely that in the 13th or 14th century, the bishop's manor house was established at Thorpe Hall, about a mile from the church. By the early 14th century, the bishop's manor house had its own chapel.

At some point in the first half of the 16th century, it was decided to move the church down what is now Thunder Lane and westwards along what is now Yarmouth Road to its present site opposite River Green (see "The Old Church and the Movement of the Settlement" above). The 1950s excavation showed that the original church was systematically destroyed in the 16th century when all walls and foundations (except those of the Norman apse) were removed.

THE THUNDER LANE / YARMOUTH ROAD JUNCTION

There have been several changes to the junction between Thunder Lane and Yarmouth Road. The first was the creation in the 16th century of the part of Yarmouth Road between Thunder Lane and just past the railway bridge (see "The Old Church and the Movement of the Settlement" above). The second was the extension in about 1700 of the garden of No. 105 (see "105 Yarmouth Road" above).

Before the 16th century, the road that Yarmouth Road met just east of Whitlingham Lane was Common Lane. Now Common Lane does not begin until the Red Lion. Until a date between 1825 and 1836 it continued westwards to the Thunder Lane junction (see Plate 32 in Appendix 2).

When the part of Yarmouth Road between Thunder Lane and just past the railway bridge was created, it did not meet the other part of Yarmouth Road at the Thunder Lane junction. Instead, the part between 68 Yarmouth Road (Roxley House) and the junction ran further to the north than today. It went north of what are now 107, 109, 111, and 113 Yarmouth Road and came out on to Thunder Lane opposite what was then the farmyard behind 105 Yarmouth Road, and is now the garage of 1 Thunder Lane. (It may then have joined a footpath that until the 18th century appears to have run behind the properties on the north side of Yarmouth Road as far west at least as the church and possibly Dale's Loke - see "Richmond Court" above). In 1769 the road was moved south to create the present junction. (It may be that, at the same, a milestone was placed next to the garden wall of 105 Yarmouth Road, opposite Whitlingham Lane. It was 2 miles from Norwich and 20 miles from Yarmouth. It was still there in the 1930s).

The junction was widened in 1959 (see "105 Yarmouth Road" above).

107, 109, 111, AND 113 YARMOUTH ROAD AND 68 YARMOUTH ROAD (ROXLEY HOUSE)

Nos. 107 and 109 are a pair of flint cottages with steep roofs. They may date from about 1700. Nos. 111 and 113 appear to date from the 19th century, although the flint in No. 111 may suggest that it incorporates an earlier building.

In 1841 the cottages were in the same ownership as 105 Yarmouth Road, on the opposite corner of Thunder Lane.

On the other side of Yarmouth Road, immediately east of Roxley Close, is 68 Yarmouth Road (Roxley House). This house dates from the 1880s and was first associated with William Thomas Fisher Jarrold, a partner in Jarrold & Sons, publishers, booksellers, printers and stationers.

Plate 24 : On the left, the sign of the Red Lion with a farm building, and on the right, Dales Place, with Common Lane and 80 onwards Yarmouth Road beyond, in about 1915.

RED LION

The Red Lion appears to have been built between 1830 and 1841. In 1841 it was in the same ownership as 105 Yarmouth Road. Opposite it is Common Lane and to east of it is School Avenue.

Where the car park now is (east of the Red Lion), there used to be farm buildings that seem to have been contemporary with the public house (Plate 24). Oral evidence suggest that, before the First World War and for a while afterwards, the Red Lion was a beer house and a common lodging house, where drovers stayed overnight. The drovers would have been bringing cattle in from the Acle marshes to Norwich market.

West of the Red Lion is 125 Yarmouth Road (Forge Cottage). It was built between 1825 and 1841. Its name suggests it was the site of a smithy, presumably linked with the farm.

Field boundaries on the 1841 tithe map suggest that there may have been a north/south track immediately west of the Red Lion. From here it may have run northwards close to what are now a north/south stretch of Meadow Lane and the southern entrance to the allotments. It may have continued northwards along the western boundary of the allotments and the original churchyard (see "The Original Church and Settlement" above) to Yarmouth Way. North of Yarmouth Way, it may have followed "the olde churche pathe" (shown on the 1585 Mousehold map) to Mousehold Heath. South of the Red Lion, the track may have joined the short north/south stretch of Common Lane, although this is slightly to the east of the suggested route of the track.

FROM THE "DALES PLACE" SIGN TO COMMON LANE
THE SITE OF THE THIRD POORHOUSE

Opposite 125 Yarmouth Road and the Red Lion and immediately west of Common Lane are some modern houses. They stand on the site of what was between 1782 and 1834 the village poorhouse or "town house". This was "for the maintenance and employment of such poor persons belonging to the parish as" were "unable to maintain themselves". An existing house was "fitted up" as a workhouse. There were two rooms on the ground floor and a chamber and garrets above. Along the east side of the building was a lean-to with a pantry and one other room on the ground floor and a large chamber above them. At the north end of the building, there was a wash-house. The premises also included a stable or outhouse, a garden and a yard.

Supple (pages 99-100) describes the life of the poor living in the town house. They were supervised by a matron. The doors were closed at 9pm and nobody was admitted after that time. If anyone got drunk or behaved in a disorderly manner, they were taken into custody by the parish constable and had to appear before a magistrate. In January 1796 the high cost of corn and other provisions led to changes in the diet of those living in the town house. Rice replaced wheat-flour and, as far as possible, potatoes replaced bread. On Mondays dinner was meat broth thickened with rice. On Wednesdays and Fridays dinner consisted of potatoes and red herrings. Where bread was given, it was made with half wheat meal and half barley flour mixed together.

In 1834 the poor living in the town house were moved to the new Union workhouse at Lingwood. The town house site was purchased by Robert Dale, a timber merchant, who built cottages there. It appears from the 1825 river map that 7 Dales Place was the site of the old town house building. A date stone in a wall reads "Dales Place 1841". By 1861 there were 13 cottages in "Dales Place" (Plate 24). In 1891 two of them had just one room, five had two rooms, one had three rooms, four had four rooms and one had at least five rooms.

At the end of the north-south stretch of Common Lane is an old wall and tucked around the corner facing the river is 12 Common Lane. This is now called Roxley Cottage but was previously called Larkhall Place. In the 1840s it was owned by John Rayner, a market gardener. He was keen to guard his property rights against his neighbour, Robert Dale. This is why there was a precise inscription on what was referred to as the Larkhall Place pillar. Today the inscription "JR 1846" can be seen on a stone in a brick pillar, probably a boundary marker.

COMMON LANE
(INCLUDING THE SITE OF THE SECOND POORHOUSE)

Common Lane may mark the original northern boundary of the common. It was also the boundary between the common pasture and the common field. The lane may have arisen in stages progressing eastwards as more of the common was enclosed. Running south from Common Lane, there was a track south of the Willows (even numbers 110-128 Yarmouth Road). This may mark an earlier edge of the common, or it may simply be an access way to the common. The earliest maps (the 1700 / 1731 sketch maps) show the western boundary of the common in the same place as it was on enclosure in 1863 i.e. the line of Bungalow Lane. Therefore Bungalow Lane may mark what had always been the boundary between common pasture (i.e. the "common") to the east and common meadow to the west. (For more on the common and how the route of Common Lane has changed, see "The Thunder Lane / Yarmouth Road Junction" above and below).

The track referred to above that ran south from Common Lane (south of the Willows) was also important in the development of Thorpe's poorhouse or "town house". In 1769 the town house moved from River Green to a site that had the track to the west and Common Lane to the north. It was divided into four tenements. As mentioned above under "From the 'Dales Place' sign to Common Lane", the town house moved again in 1782.

80-94B (EVEN NUMBERS) YARMOUTH ROAD

THE SITE OF A TANNERY

These houses, opposite what is now School Avenue, mark the former site of a tannery. In 1800 it was described as a "House with Tan office, outbuildings, Cottages, Yards and Gardens" owned by Jane Smith, occupied by William Smith and of 1.329 acres. The 1825 river map shows a large building on the site, that may have been a drying shed.

An 1830 directory lists William Smith and Thomas Batley, both of Thorpe, as tanners. Smith seems to have been operating from this site and Batley from the site north of 105 Yarmouth Road. Norwich Castle Museum & Art Gallery has a watercolour by John Thirtle called "*A Tanyard, Thorpe near Norwich*". It was first exhibited in 1808. It appears to be of Smith's tanyard since the road slopes down in front of the tanyard, which is on the right of the road. Smith's tannery had gone by 1841 and Batley's probably by 1845.

V: From Thorpe Mews to Primrose Crescent

110-128 (EVEN NUMBERS) YARMOUTH ROAD (THE WILLOWS) AND THE CEMETERY

In 1825 there were no buildings on either side of the road between what is now 80-94B (even numbers) Yarmouth Road and the railway bridge. The position was the same in 1841 and only slightly different by the 1880s. By then, on the south side of the road, were a cemetery and a terrace called the Willows.

The churchyard ceased to be used for burials in 1858, when an acre of land was purchased as a cemetery and, in the following year, a small mortuary chapel was built (Plate 25). The cost was £250. At the same time, the asylum (see "St Andrew's Park" below) purchased the same amount of land for use as a cemetery immediately west of the church's plot. The chapel was demolished in 1973. The cemetery was extended eastwards in 1977.

Plate 25 : Thorpe cemetery and mortuary chapel in about 1905.

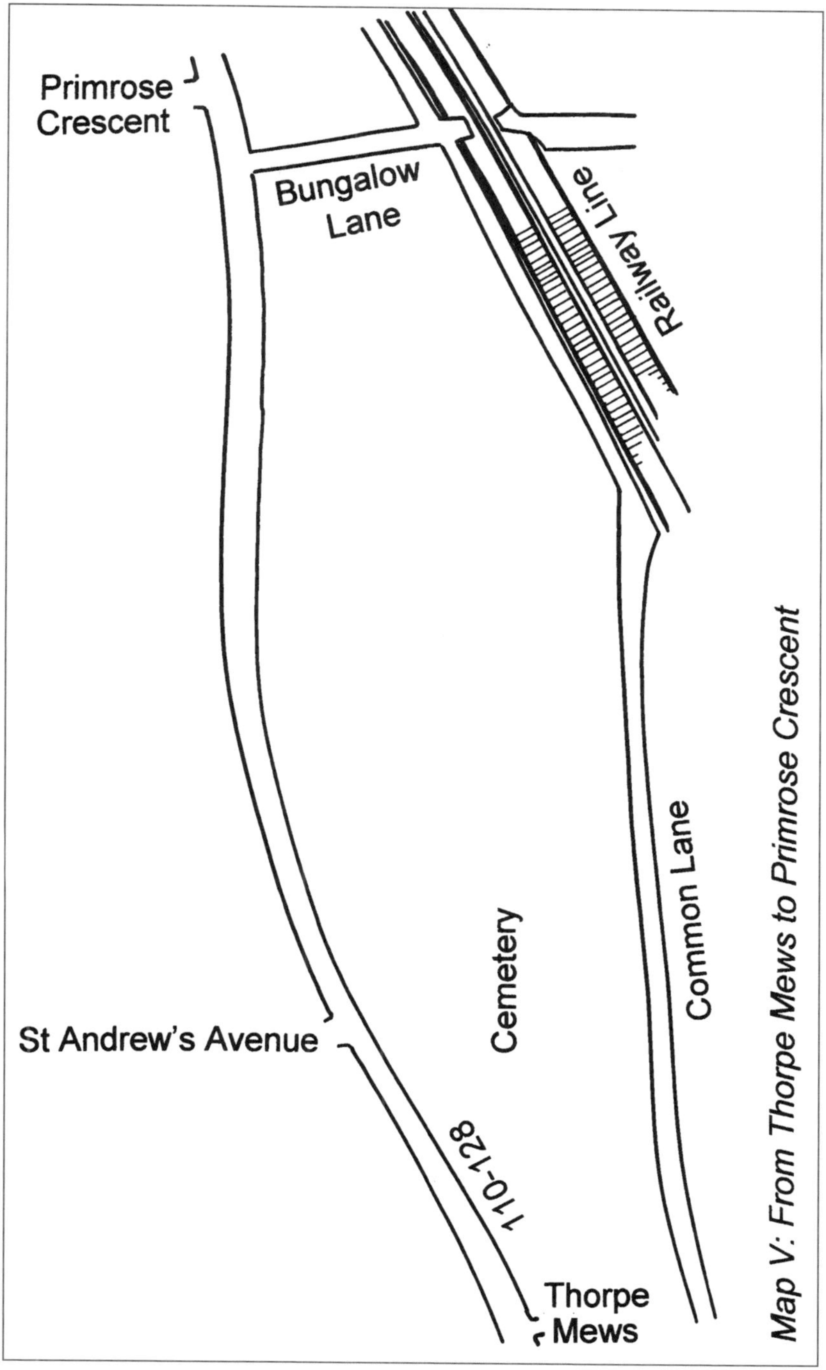

Map V: From Thorpe Mews to Primrose Crescent

BUNGALOW LANE AND THE COMMON

The common was known as the Low or Wet Common, as distinct from the high and dry common of Mousehold Heath. As mentioned above under "Common Lane", Bungalow Lane formed the western boundary of the common from at least the early 18th century until the common was enclosed in 1863. The common extended eastwards to Boundary Lane and a ditch that formed Thorpe's eastern boundary. The southern boundary of the common was the river. The northern boundary was just behind the properties fronting Yarmouth Road.

Under an 1803 agreement, there were 89 "goings" or rights to graze a beast on the common. Rights were attached to certain properties. For example, in 1741, John Bunting, the tenant of the King's Head, had the right to pasture two beasts on the common. However, by 1810, common rights were being sold separately from properties.

Horses, cows and one or two bulls were allowed to graze on the common from 13 May until the following 1 February. On these days the parish bells rang between nine and twelve in the morning to signify the beginning or ending of the grazing season. There were two ways into or out of the common. One was along Common Lane, the other was next to what is now the northern end of Griffin Lane. It seems likely from the 1841 tithe map that this northern entrance used to be a wide way immediately west of Griffin Lane.

The 1841 tithe map also shows that by this time the common was divided into four pieces - a major section of just over 60 acres, a riverside stretch of just over 6 acres and smaller pieces of 1.2 and 0.5 acres. The 89 common rights were divided among 11 common right owners. The two major owners were Sarah Batley with 24 rights and John Harvey with 21.

In 1843/4 the new Norwich to Yarmouth railway line was built across the common.

In 1863 the common was enclosed and divided amongst those who had rights over it. What is now Griffin Lane was extended eastwards to give access to the new enclosures. Another new road (Bungalow Lane) was built along what had been the western edge of the common.

In 1865 work began on the new railway line between Norwich and North Walsham. Work was halted in 1866 and was not completed until 1874. The line was built to the west of the old common and led to the diversion of Common Lane away from the common and along the north-western side of the railway track.

At the time of the 1871 census, there were families living in 5 tents on the former common. There was a travelling musician, a brazier, a hawker, a horse dealer and a cane chair mender.

VI: From Pound Lane to the Griffin

POUND LANE

Pound Lane was built in 1801 as a private road between the newly-created fields on what until then had been Mousehold Heath. Before 1801 the heath began just south of where the Ring Road now joins Pound Lane. Immediately south of the Sainsbury's site is where Yarmouth Way would have crossed what is now Pound Lane and then continued east-south-eastwards to the other side of what is now the railway bridge.

When it was first built Pound Lane did not continue southwards as now but followed the edge of Mousehold Heath south-eastwards until it met Yarmouth Road. By the 1830s this route had been abandoned and the present southern route established. Until the late 1860s, Pound Lane continued further southwards than now, meeting Yarmouth Road behind what is now Rowena Terrace (even numbers 196-206 Yarmouth Road).

On the eastern side of the junction with Yarmouth Road was the village pound, a small rectangular enclosure where stray animals were confined and only released on payment of a fine. In 1868 the pound was offered to the East Norfolk Railway Company for £40. This was in connection with the building of the new railway line to North Walsham and the consequent movement further northwards of the part of Yarmouth Road that had previously run in a straight line east-north-eastwards from Bungalow Lane to just east of the railway bridge.

Nearly a mile along Pound Lane is the Oasis Sports and Leisure Centre. This was formerly "The Woodlands". It dates from about 1860 and is first associated with Charles Jecks, a timber merchant. In 1864 it was described as "pleasantly situated in well wooded grounds in which is a small lake".

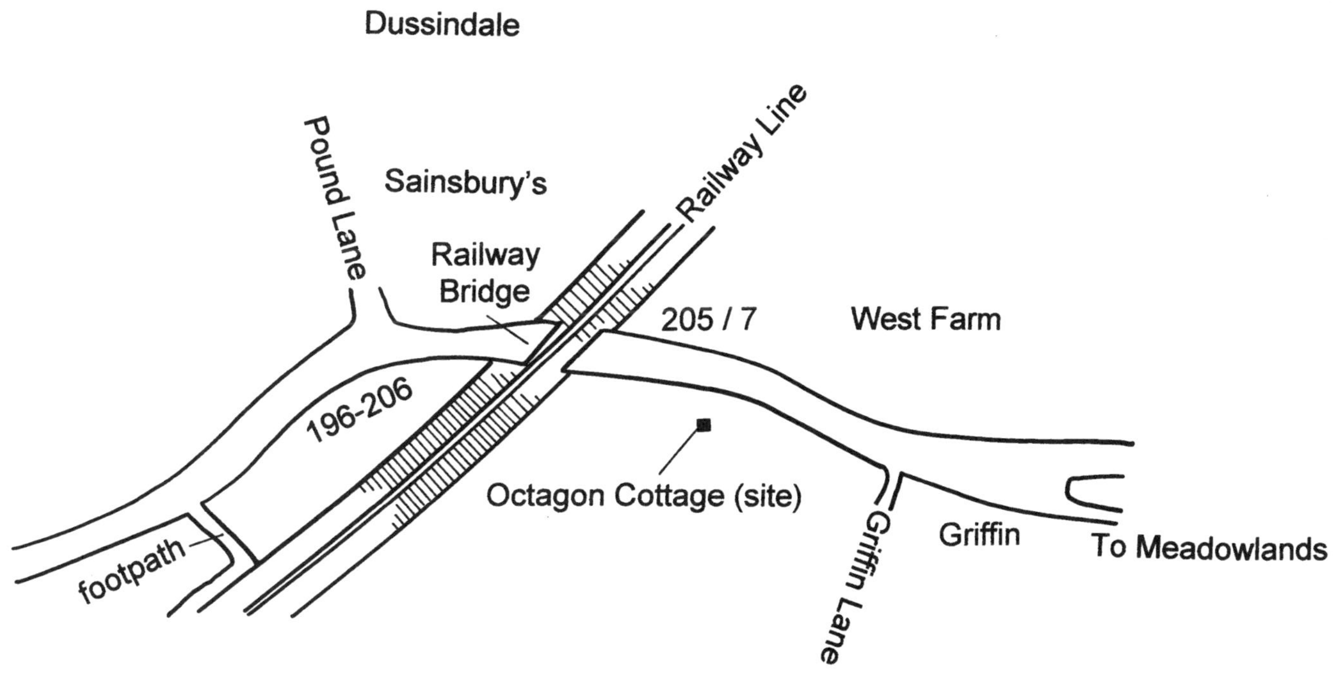

Map VI: From Pound Lane to the Griffin

SAINSBURY'S AND DUSSINDALE

The Sainsbury's supermarket was opened in 1989 and a new community centre, the Dussindale Centre, in 1990. Before 1801 the site was part of Mousehold Heath. By 1810 there was a marl pit and a limekiln there. At a manor court in 1836, a complaint was made that, since acquiring the site in 1820, John Harvey had dug and sold "divers quantities of Marle" from the land and had "burnt divers quantities of chalk into lime and sold the same without permission." In 1938-9 the site of a Romano-British pottery kiln was discovered. It was dated to the early second century.

North of Sainsbury's, between Pound Lane and the railway line, is a modern housing development called Dussindale Park. "Dussindale" was the site of the final battle of Kett's rebellion in 1549 where the rebels were defeated. The battle did not take place where the houses now are. Anne Carter has shown that there was a Dussindale (Dussings Deale) nearby, but it was on the other side of the railway line to the housing development, west of Green Lane South. (Before the recent building of Norwich's southern bypass, Green Lane South continued southwards to what is now the southern end of Old Chapel Way). It also seems that this was not the only Dussindale in the area and so it is not the only possible site of the battle.

In about 1720 Kirkpatrick drew a plan of the earthworks of St William's Chapel, Mousehold Heath, between Mousehold Lane and Gurney Road. He annotated the plan with notes, including a statement that the chapel was about 260 paces north of Dussindale (Dussyns Dale). Since he said that ten of his paces equalled about nine yards (eight metres), it means Dussindale was about 234 yards (214 metres) south of the chapel site. This takes you to just north of where Valley Drive joins Gurney Road. It suggests that he thought Dussindale was the valley that runs west along Valley Drive, north across Gurney Road and then west through Long Valley to Gilman Road. Further weight to this suggestion is given by the fact that Kirkpatrick was a meticulous historian who was particularly interested in place-names. There is evidence to suggest that the "Valley Drive Dussindale" is a more likely site for the battle than the "Green Lane South Dussindale".

Sotherton's contemporary account of the battle says it was "not past a mile away" from the rebels' camp. The rebels' camp was near the top of Gas Hill. Valley Drive is less than a mile away. Green Lane South is almost three miles away. The indictment against Kett said that Dussindale was in "the parishes of Sprowston and Thorpe". Green Lane South is on the border of the parishes of Thorpe, Postwick and Plumstead. Valley Drive is very close to the old boundary between Thorpe and Sprowston, which used to run approximately along the line of what is now Rider Haggard Road, a road on the opposite side of Heartsease Lane to Valley Drive.

205 AND 207 YARMOUTH ROAD, WEST FARM (213 AND 215 YARMOUTH ROAD), THE GRIFFIN AND THE SITE OF OCTAGON COTTAGE

On the east side of the railway bridge, on the north side of the road, are 205 and 207 Yarmouth Road. They are a pair of brick and tile cottages with a half-flint gable end. They date from the early 19th century. Until the 1990s, on the opposite side of the road to them was a curious octagonal building that was called Octagon Cottage or the Round House (Plate 26). In 1803 it was described as "a new cottage built on land belonging to Sir Roger Kerrison". It was a double cottage of flint and red brick with pointed "Gothic-style" windows and doors. It was reputed to be a toll-house. It certainly looked like one and there is strong circumstantial evidence that, when it was built, in the late 18th century, this was its function.

Octagon Cottage was built at a very important road junction and next to where the common met Mousehold Heath. Enclosure, road diversions and road closures have altered very much how the area looked just over 200 years ago (see Plate 32 in Appendix 2).

Before Mousehold Heath was enclosed in 1801, the heath came down to the road between what is now the boundary between 207 and 209 Yarmouth Road and the eastern edge of the farm buildings (i.e. West Farm formerly Lime Kiln Farm now 213 and 215 Yarmouth Road). Yarmouth Way came down from the west-north-west and reached what is now Yarmouth Road also near the boundary between 207 and 209 Yarmouth Road. Yarmouth Road came up from the west-south-west emerging just south of the railway bridge and reaching the present Yarmouth Road just west of what was Octagon Cottage, close to where Yarmouth Way came down from the west-north-west. Cutting between the heath to the north and the way to the common to the south, Yarmouth Road followed its present course until immediately past West Farm. Here, it went past the present site of the Griffin and continued east-south-eastwards, passing just 30 yards (27 metres) from what became the front of the main buildings of St Andrew's Hospital (see "St Andrew's Park" below).

Yarmouth Way was closed in 1801. Within a few years, a single storey flint and brick double cottage (the predecessor of 209 and 211 Yarmouth Road) and farm buildings had been built across where Mousehold Heath had met Yarmouth Road. The Griffin moved to its present site in 1846, having previously been situated east of St Andrew's Hospital. The part of Yarmouth Road that continued beyond the Griffin changed to its present route in 1856. The part of Yarmouth Road that came from the west changed to its present route in the 1860s.

Octagon Cottage was probably a toll-house. Its faceted design meant that windows faced both ways along the road. This would enable a toll-keeper to see traffic coming and open the gate or bar that presumably adjoined the house. Yarmouth Road was a turnpike road from 1769. The 1825 river map shows that at that time, the toll-bar was across the road at the far eastern end of the parish, the boundary with Postwick. However, until Yarmouth Way was closed in 1801, it would not have been possible to have a toll-gate there, because it would have blocked

Plate 26 : Octagon Cottage in the 1960s.

access to Yarmouth Way. The ideal place for a toll-bar would have been immediately west of where Yarmouth Way joined Yarmouth Road. This was where Octagon Cottage was situated and so, from the late 18th century until 1801, it is very likely that it was the toll-house.

Octagon Cottage was last occupied in 1963. It then fell into disrepair. By 1987 only part of one wall was standing. Now there is very little of it left.

Plate 27 : On the right, the sign of the Griffin and, beyond that, the nurses' home (now Meadowlands) and the asylum, in about 1915.

VII: From Meadowlands to Boundary Lane

ST ANDREW'S BUSINESS PARK
FORMERLY PART OF ST ANDREW'S HOSPITAL

East of West Farm, on the north side of the road, was a large enclosed field known in 1585 as "Readings Close" and owned by Edward Paston, lord of the manor of Thorpe. The name suggests the field was taken in from the heath or woodland. The field extended almost as far east as the parish boundary. Part of the field "moved" to the other side of the road when Yarmouth Road was moved northwards in the 1850s. At the same time what was left of the field, and fields to the north became the asylum farm. The area now forms part of St Andrew's Business Park.

North of what was Readings Close and at the end of what is now Northside is St Andrew's House, the headquarters of the Norfolk Health Authority. This was formerly the northern annex of St Andrew's Hospital (previously the County Lunatic Asylum) – see "St Andrew's Park" below. It was built in 1880 and extended in 1903.

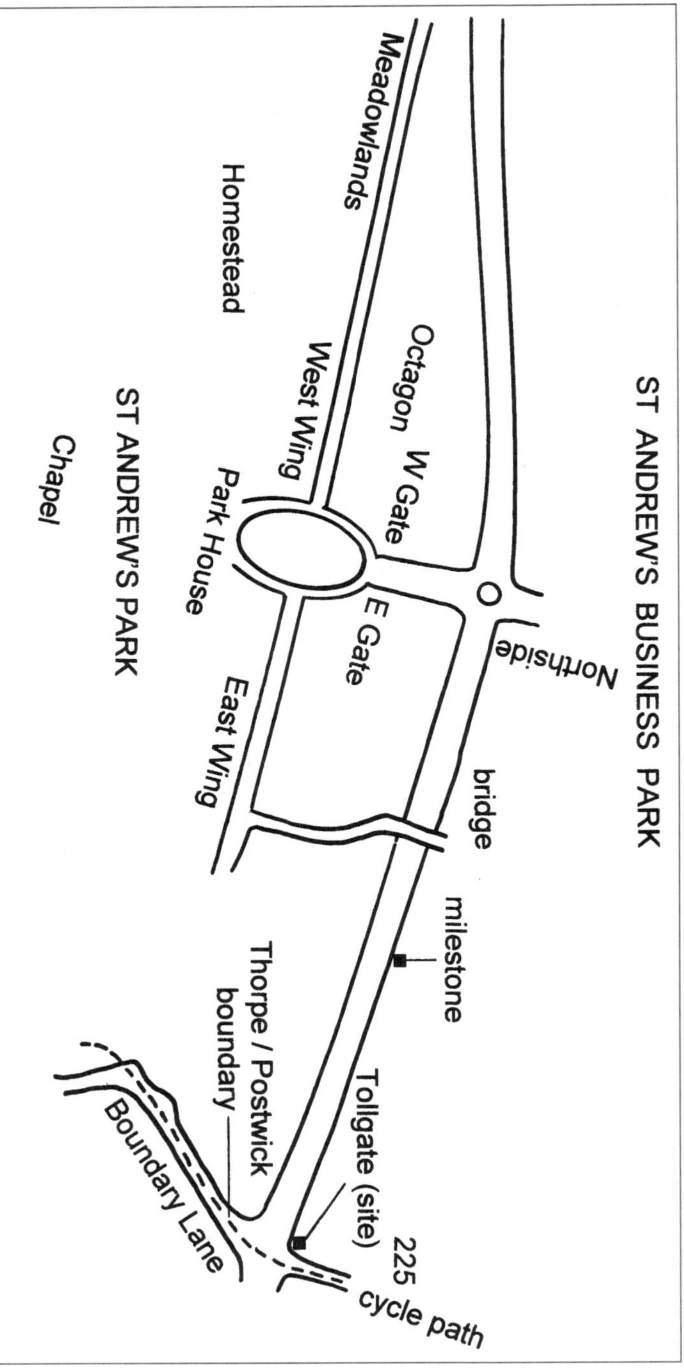

Map VII: From Meadowlands to Boundary Lane

ST ANDREW'S PARK

FORMERLY ST ANDREW'S HOSPITAL AND PREVIOUSLY THE COUNTY LUNATIC ASYLUM

Description

On the south side of road is what is now called St Andrew's Park. The recent redevelopment of this site as a residential area has included refurbishment of many of the buildings that were part of the 19th century asylum.

The "East Gate" and "West Gate" were lodges on either side of the asylum entrance. They were built in 1867. One was used as the doctor's stable.

West of the West Gate, "The Octagon" dates from about 1900. Since it was next to, and provided workers for, the laundry, it was originally called "Laundry Ward". Later it became a recreational and entertainment centre. In 1974 it was named the Octagon Centre after Octagon Cottage (see "205 and 207 Yarmouth Road etc" above).

South of East Gate and West Gate are the principal surviving buildings.

Plate 28 : County Lunatic Asylum, Thorpe, Norfolk, from a drawing by J B Ladbrooke of about 1825.

What are now 1-18 Park House, 12-13 East Wing and 8-9 West Wing was the original asylum of 1812-1814, although with later modifications. For example, the south side of the central section was modified in the late 1870s.

The southern halves of the cross-wings date from about 1830, although they may have been modified in 1842. (They are now 14 East Wing and 10 West Wing).When they were built, they extended further southwards than now. The northern halves of the cross-wings date from 1842. (They are now 9-11 East Wing and 5-7 West Wing). Their northern ends abutted on what was then Yarmouth Road.

The lateral extensions at the northern ends of the cross-wings date from the late 1850s, although they have been modified. (They are now 2-8 East Wing and 1-4 West Wing). 15 East Wing and 11 West Wing appear to date from about 1880, although the former is on the site of a part of the building that was erected in 1842 and the latter is on the site of part of the building that was erected in 1830.

West of the West Wing, "The Homestead" dates from about 1880. It used to be where some of the wards were.

South of the main buildings is the asylum chapel, now converted into two dwellings. The octagonal part of it dates from the late 1850s. The nave that adjoins it was added in about 1880, as was the bell-tower. East of the chapel and south of 14 East Wing, there was a burial ground that was in use from 1814 until 1858.

History

In 1811 it was decided to erect a new asylum in Norfolk. The plans of William Brown, an Ipswich architect, were accepted. Detailed drawings were made by Francis Stone, the County Surveyor. Five acres of freehold land in Thorpe were purchased at a cost of £600. Building work began early in 1812 and, in May 1814, according to the Norfolk Chronicle, "Thorpe asylum was opened for the reception of forty male pauper lunatics." A few months later, female patients were admitted.

The asylum was built to accommodate 100 patients. It consisted of a central three-storey block for the officers and for administrative purposes, with two-storey wings extending east and west. The eastern wing was for female patients and the western wing was for the men.

Thomson, who wrote a brief history in 1903, described the original asylum:- "There was a 12 feet (3.5 metres) to 15 feet (4.5 metres) wall round the whole building. The few windows there were, were all iron-barred and grilled. The dormitories and single rooms were called cells. They were almost dark, paved with stone with a drain gulley in the middle of the floor, lighted at night by lanterns in which fish oil was burnt. What little heavy furniture there was, was fixed to the floor. The bedding was a litter of straw on which the inmates lay chained like wild beasts. The cutlery was of wood or bone and there were tin mugs and platters."

The 1825 river map shows a walled courtyard behind the asylum with a few small buildings outside that. Chambers, in 1829, described it as "a noble erection of white (sic) brick, the extent of front being no less than 430 feet (131 metres), with a portico in the centre, supported by four columns. The

Plate 29 : Thorpe Asylum in about 1905.

lowest apartments, or cellars, are covered with a circular vaulting, which sustains the rest of the building. The stone staircase is particularly worthy of notice, from the lightness and strength of its construction; it is of the well form and lighted at the top with a lantern."

There is an engraving of a J B Ladbrooke drawing of the asylum that was published in 1825 (Plate 28). It shows a Classical front with a seven bay three-storey centre block with the central three bays projecting under a pediment, with a portico. On either side of the centre block there was a two storey wing of 16 bays, some projecting. (Apart from one bay at either end, the frontage of the building survives intact as "Park House" – see "Description" above). Not far from the front of the building was a wall with railings that separated the asylum from the road. The engraving shows how close to the building Yarmouth Road used to be.

In about 1830 the asylum was enlarged to accommodate 25 more patients on the male and female sides. The 1841 tithe map shows that this was done by building extensions and southern cross-wings at the eastern and western ends. Also, by 1841, there was a range of buildings south of the male side of the asylum and the same on the female side. They included a wash-house and a chapel. The courtyard between these southern buildings and the asylum was split by a series of divisions that separated the hospital officials from the patients, separated different groups of patients from one another and linked groups of patients to parts of the southern buildings.

In 1841 it was reported that the asylum was crowded, especially on the female (i.e. eastern) side. This led to further extensions of the buildings that were completed in 1842. According to White's Norfolk of 1845, the asylum had accommodation for "more than 200 patients, of whom it has generally upwards of 150, who are maintained at the average weekly cost of 5s $9^1/_2$d per head for the pauper lunatics and 10s for boarders".

It is clear from a plan of January 1854 that the 1842 changes involved modification of the cross-wings. They were extended northwards so their northern ends abutted on what was then Yarmouth Road. The 1854 plan shows that, by that date, south of the central section of the main building was a chapel. (This appears to have been partly under the nave and partly under the chancel of the later chapel). South of the eastern wing of the main building was a drying ground. South of the eastern cross-wing was a burial ground.

In 1844 three acres was purchased on the west side of the asylum. Two years later, in 1846, 2.5 acres were acquired on the east side of the asylum. The latter included the site of the early 19th century Griffin public house. This was then pulled down and rebuilt in its present location west of the asylum. By early 1854 the newly acquired land had become a garden for the male patients on the west side of the asylum and a recreation area and a garden for the women on the east side of the building.

Steadily growing numbers of patients at the asylum meant increasing demand for space. In July 1852 plans for extending the wings of the asylum were approved provided additional space could be obtained for the exercise and employment of patients. In 1853 30 acres were purchased on the north side of Yarmouth Road - from just west of where Northside now is to Green Lane South. (The latter used to continue southwards to what is now the southern end of Old Chapel Way). A similar amount of land west of Northside was leased from the Earl of Rosebery. The new land was used as an asylum farm, where patients were employed. In the plans for extending the asylum, it was proposed to provide additional accommodation for 139 patients, a new chapel, a new laundry and drying houses with requisite apparatus. The plans included a new system to supply sufficient water, a new drainage system, apparatus for warming, ventilating and lighting and a dining room "of ample dimensions".

It was not possible to expand southwards because of the common and the unsuitable ground. To expand northwards, the road would have to be moved. Before the enlargement scheme could be approved, a diversion of Yarmouth Road had to be agreed. In January 1854 it was proposed to divert Yarmouth Road so that it ran to the south of the hospital. The turnpike trustees rejected this, because it would mean a longer road and a steep ascent at the western end. It would also interfere with the consecrated burial ground at the asylum. In March 1854 a proposal to divert the turnpike to the north of the asylum was accepted provided the diversion continued further at the western end than had been suggested.

Work on the new road was completed in 1856. At its furthest point the new road was 100 yards (91 metres) from the front of the hospital. The old road had been 30 yards (27 metres) away. The excavated earth formed fortification-like mounds in front of the asylum. Also, in 1856, a new permanent bridge was built across the road "for the convenience of the workmen on the farm". The bridge still exists. It replaced a temporary footbridge over the road that was built in 1855.

About 40 yards (37 metres) east of the bridge, there is a milestone against the wall on the north side of the road. Presumably this also dates from 1856, although it may have been moved from the old road. It records the fact that it is 3 miles from Norwich and 19 miles from Yarmouth.

As the new road was completed, work on the new asylum buildings began. A new laundry, east and west towers for water storage in case of fire, and new workshops were built between the new road and what had been the old road. Near the east tower, a slaughter-house was built. Next door to it was a building where vegetables were cooked. Just east of the bridge across from the farm, there was a reservoir. New blocks of wards were added by lateral extensions at the northern ends of the cross-wings of the main asylum building. South of it an octagonal chapel was built. A new dining hall was also erected.

In the 1860s and 1870s further changes were made. In 1861 farm buildings were erected on the asylum's land to the north of the road. The lodges at the entrance to the asylum were added in 1867 (Plate 29). Extra wards were added to the female side of the asylum in 1869 and 1873. Two wards on the male side were extended in 1876.

Thomson records that "in 1880, further additions to the existing buildings being impossible, the committee decided to build an Annex or Auxiliary Asylum on land to the north of the Main Asylum, about 500 yards (457 metres) away. The Annex would be a plain, simple and comparatively cheap building to house quiet and tractable chronic cases. It would contain 280 beds, 140 of each sex." The Annex is now "St Andrew's House".

The original asylum was in yellow brick and the extensions to it in "white" brick. It was decided that the new asylum should be in red brick. According to White's Norfolk of 1883, the new building was "after the design of R M Phipson of Norwich" and consisted of "two large wards for males and females, with dormitories, baths and all requisites... The airing court or garden where the patients take recreation comprises an acre and a half of ground, tastefully laid out with flowerbeds, shrubs, drinking fountains etc."

Also in 1880, a nave was added to the octagonal chapel at the old asylum. At the same time, a bell-tower was erected next to the octagonal part of the chapel.

Between 1885 and 1912 accommodation was built for staff outside the asylums. In the 1880s and 1890s a row of eighteen attendants' cottages was erected on the north side of Yarmouth Road, next to the Thorpe boundary, but just into Postwick. They were known as the "Norfolk Cottages". (They were demolished in 1997). In 1892 a large house was built for the medical superintendent. This was also on the north side of Yarmouth Road, but just within Thorpe. Until 1892, the superintendent had been housed in uncomfortable and inadequate quarters in the centre of the old asylum. His new house was known as "Thorpe End". (It was also pulled down in the 1990s).

There were major changes at the asylum in 1903. The main purpose was to provide extra accommodation for the male patients. The old asylum would now just be for female patients and the new asylum just for the men. The changes included building a road to the new asylum (now Northside) and increasing accommodation there by constructing a large south-west extension. The whole asylum would contain 1000 beds – 550 at the old or women's asylum and 450 at the new or men's asylum.

At the old asylum, a new boiler house and central generating station was built on the east side, including subways for water mains. Work included the construction of a chimney, 110 feet high (33.5 metres), next to the boiler house. (The chimney was demolished in 1977).

A 1903 description of the old or women's asylum describes what the complex was like. The central administrative block consisted of a board room, where the monthly meetings of the committees were held; offices for the medical superintendent, the clerk and the steward; quarters and mess for the assistant medical officers and matrons; a dispensary; steward's stores and visiting room. Buildings stretching east and west consisted of wards; laundry; kitchens; chapel; recreation hall; nurses' mess rooms and bedrooms; fire station: engineer's and clerk of works' departments; stables and coach-houses; and the sewage works.

In 1910 a nurses' home for 50 nurses was built on the west side of the old asylum, near the Griffin (Plate 27). (It is now known as Meadowlands). In 1912 a new recreation hall was erected south-east of the central administrative block.

In April 1915 the asylum was converted into a military hospital – the Norfolk War Hospital (Plate 30). Repeated extensions of the hospital buildings

Plate 30 : Norfolk War Hospital in about 1915.

became necessary, and the institution came to contain about 2,450 beds for sick and wounded soldiers. There were three divisions – the main hospital, the annexe hospital and the camp (situated behind the annexe). Thorpe Hospital was the central hospital in Norfolk to the fifty auxiliary (or VAD) hospitals scattered throughout the county. It was officially closed in April 1919. In 1920 Earl Haig unveiled a plaque in the entrance hall of the hospital, recording that 45,000 military patients had been treated there between 1915 and 1919.

In 1920 the asylum changed its name to the Norfolk Mental Hospital and in 1925 the name changed again to St Andrew's Hospital.

The hospital closed in the summer of 1998. The north side of the site is being redeveloped as St. Andrew's Business Park and the south side is being turned into a prestigious housing development, St Andrew's Park.

225 YARMOUTH ROAD, BOUNDARY LANE AND THE SITE OF THE TOLLGATE

The last house in Thorpe is 225 Yarmouth Road. (It is now boarded up). South of this, by the roadside, until the 1960s, there was a house called "Sunflower Cottage". It was reconstructed and re-roofed in 1900, when it was the house of the resident engineer to the asylum (see "St Andrew's Park" above). Before it was largely rebuilt, it was an early 19th century cottage that in 1888 was referred to as "Old Tollgate House". From about 1801 until about 1840, it was here at the boundary between Thorpe and Postwick that there was a toll-bar across the road, known as Postwick Gate.

In about 1840 this was replaced by a tollgate at the western extremity of Thorpe. The latter went across from what is now the Canton Chinese Restaurant, 129 Thorpe Road, but was previously the Redan. It was called the Thorpe Gate and remained in use until 1874, when tolls were abolished, the toll-house was demolished and the Redan public house was built on the site. (Midway between what was the Redan and Telegraph Lane East, on the north side of the road, there used to be milestone that was 1 mile from Norwich and 21 miles from Yarmouth).

East of 225 Yarmouth Road is a cycle path that initially follows what was the northern side of Boundary Lane, the parish boundary between Thorpe and Postwick. On the south side of Yarmouth Road, the boundary goes south-westwards along part of what still is Boundary Lane and then continues south-south-westwards along a ditch to the river.

From where a railway bridge crosses Low Road, Plumstead southwards to the river, the parish boundary followed a stream referred to in a river survey of 1767 as Muck Fleet. On the west side of that railway bridge, there was a farm known as Brook Farm. By the 18th century it was leased from Norwich Cathedral as part of Lumner's Foldcourse, which used to belong to the Cathedral Priory. It was demolished in about 1997 to make way for an extension to the Dussindale housing development.

Appendix 1 Thorpe Manor

Lordship of the Manor until 1536

The first-recorded lord of the manor of Thorpe was Stigand who was head of Edward the Confessor's secretariat and bishop of East Anglia in 1042. Stigand was probably granted Thorpe by Edward the Confessor in 1042, although he may have received it earlier since he had been an influential royal adviser since at least 1020, when he was priest to King Cnut. According to the Anglo-Saxon Chronicle, in 1043, Edward turned against his mother (Emma) and against Stigand, his mother's "closest confidant" and adviser. Stigand lost his bishopric and lands, but they were restored to him later that year. He held the bishopric until 1047 and lands (including Thorpe) until 1070, when he fell from favour and William I confiscated his property. Stigand was Archbishop of Canterbury from 1052 until 1070 and as such appears in the Bayeux Tapestry at the coronation of King Harold in 1066.

Thorpe may be an early royal manor. There is support for this from place-name evidence. Bishopgate leads to Bishop Bridge, the lowest fording point on the Wensum and probably where a Roman road crossed the river on its way to Brundall. Ayers has suggested that within the Cathedral Close and near the river-crossing was the site of a small Middle Saxon settlement (probably of the 8th century) which can be identified with the place-name "Conesford", meaning King's ford, because it led to the King's manor of Thorpe. The reference in the Domesday Book to "woodland for 1200 pigs" suggests that Thorpe had the largest wood in Norfolk. According to Williamson, "most of the largest totals of woodland were attached to places which had been ancient estate centres, especially those which had remained in royal hands" and/or were the centres of hundreds. Since there is no evidence of Thorpe being the centre of a hundred, the size of the wood supports the idea that it was the ancient centre of a royal estate.

Of the 11 villages that surrounded Mousehold before it was enclosed in 1801, Thorpe is the only village whose Domesday Book entry mentions significant woodland. No other Mousehold parish seems to have had woodland for more than 15 pigs. The disparity between Thorpe and the other Mousehold parishes may suggest that the Thorpe part of Mousehold had received some special, perhaps royal, protection which had stopped it turning into a treeless heath.

After Stigand lost the manor of Thorpe in 1070, William I granted it to Earl Ralph de Guader. In 1075 the manor passed back to the King, as a result of the Earl's rebellion. It remained in the hands of the Crown until 1101 when Henry I granted it to Bishop Herbert.

Lordship of the Manor from 1536

By an Act of Parliament passed in 1536, Henry VIII seized most of the lands of the Bishop of Norwich (including Thorpe) and granted him in exchange the estates of St Benet's abbey.

In 1544 Henry granted the manor of Thorpe to Thomas, Duke of Norfolk with remainder to his son Henry, Earl of Surrey. Two years earlier, Surrey had obtained a lease of St Leonard's Priory, which he was pulling down and replacing with a great house that became known as Mount Surrey. The acquisition of the manor of Thorpe was probably regarded as a logical extension of this endeavour. However, three years after acquiring Thorpe, the Duke of Norfolk and the Earl of Surrey were convicted of treason. Their property passed to the Crown. Surrey was executed.

In July 1547, Henry granted the manor of Thorpe to Sir Thomas Paston, a member of the King's Privy Chamber. Sir Thomas had married Agnes, daughter and heiress of Sir John Leigh of Addington, Surrey. When Sir Thomas died, in 1550, Thorpe passed to his son Edward, who was then just a few months old. Edward attained age 21 in 1571. By his second wife, Margaret, daughter of Henry Berney of Reedham, Edward had six sons and three daughters. In 1608 Edward's eldest son, Thomas, married Mary, daughter of Sir George Browne, the second son of Viscount Montague. Under the terms of a settlement, Edward agreed that Thorpe (with Paston and Blofield, several marshes and other property in Norfolk and Suffolk) would pass to Thomas on Edward's death. (Edward also settled Binham and Barney on Thomas and Mary). Thomas died in 1622, eight years before his father. Edward died in 1630 and was remembered on his tablet in Blofield church as "most skillfull of liberal sciences especially musicke and poetry as also strange languages". Under the settlement, the manor then passed to Edward's grandson, Clement, who was then under 21. Clement, like his grandfather, was a strong Catholic. As a result, when the Civil War began in 1642, Clement's land was sequestered which meant that all income and profits went to Parliament and its soldiers. Thorpe was released from sequestration in 1656 and Clement sold the manor to Revd. Nathan Wright, a Norwich prebend. Clement died in 1662.

By 1670 the manor was in the hands of Rowland Dee, a London merchant. In 1720 his son's widow sold it to Matthew Howard, another London merchant. He died in 1737 and in 1751 his two daughters sold the manor to Thomas Vere, a worsted manufacturer who was mayor of Norwich in 1735 and an MP for Norwich from 1735 until 1747. On Thomas' death in 1766, the manor passed to his son John Vere . In 1790 John Vere died without children and, under the terms of his father's will, the manor passed to his father's "much Esteemed Friend", Thomas Lobb Chute of South Pickenham. Nine months later, in November 1790, Thomas Lobb Chute died. The manor then passed to his son, Revd. Thomas Vere Chute of the Vyne, Hampshire .

Between 1802 and 1803 Thomas Vere Chute sold off the estate attached to the manor. Sir Roger Kerrison bought most of it. Chute retained the lordship of the manor. When he died, in 1827, William Lyde Wiggett succeeded him and changed his name to Wiggett Chute. He was the second son of Chute's cousin, Revd. James Wiggett. In 1836 the lordship of the manor passed to James Cuddon, who died in 1851. In 1861 it passed from the Cuddon family to William Birkbeck. On his death in 1897, he was succeeded by his son William John Birkbeck. He died in 1916, whereupon the manor passed to the trustees of his will.

Appendix 2 – Maps of Thorpe St Andrew in about 1600 and about 1750

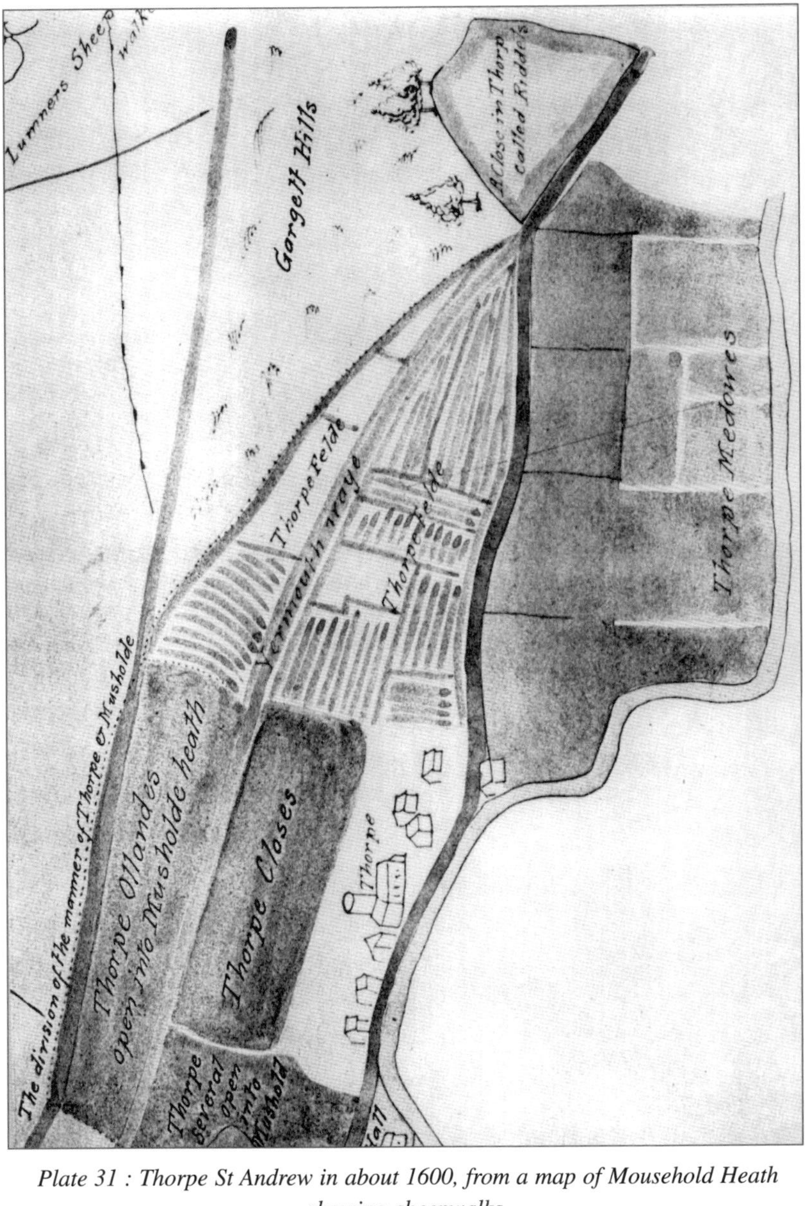

Plate 31 : Thorpe St Andrew in about 1600, from a map of Mousehold Heath showing sheepwalks.

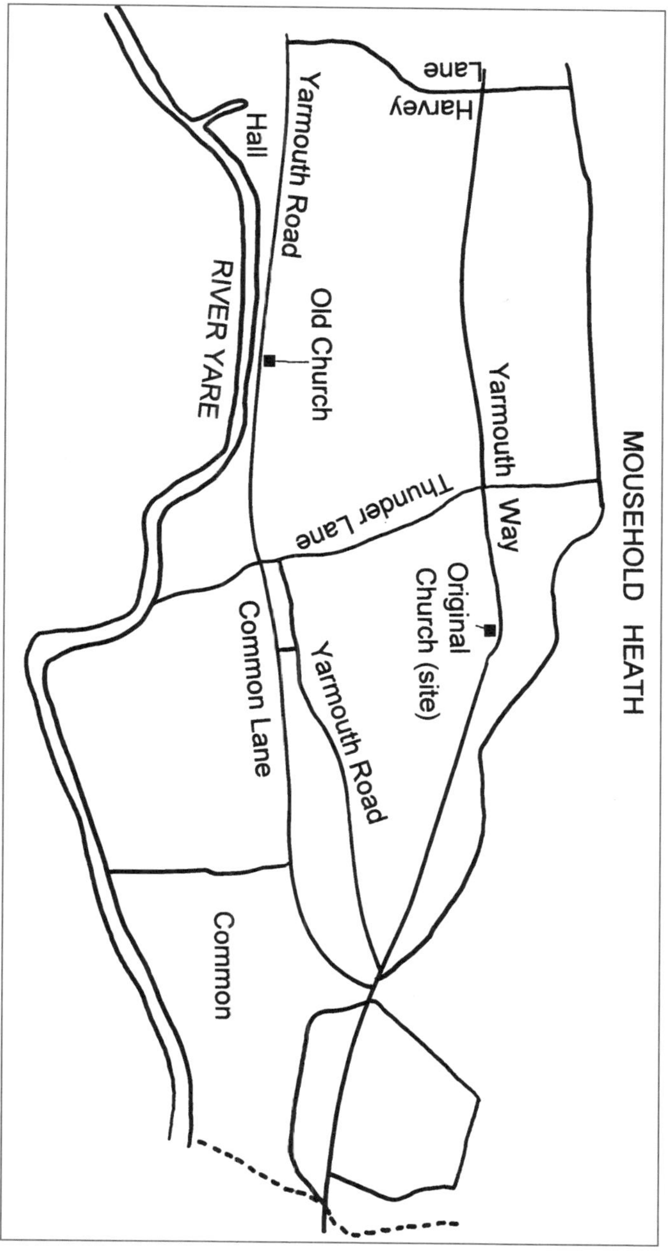

Plate 32 : Thorpe St Andrew in about 1750, showing the extent of Mousehold Heath and the common in the 18th century and the road network as it was from the mid-16th century until 1769.

Appendix 3 - Sources

Books

Aldous D W Unpublished notes of 1951-53 excavation of what until 1988 was thought to be "St Catherine's, Thorpe"

Allthorpe-Guyton M *John Thirtle (1777-1839) Drawings in Norwich Castle Museum* (1977)

Armstrong M J *History and antiquities of the county of Norfolk* (1781)

Ayers B *The Cathedral Site before 1096* in Atherton I and others (editors) *Norwich Cathedral - Church, City and Diocese 1096-1996* (1996)

Barton T F and Farrow M A (editors) *Index of wills proved in the Consistory Court of Norwich 1687-1750* Norfolk Record Society 34 (1965)

Batcock N *The Ruined and Deserted Churches of Norfolk* East Anglian Archaeology Report 51 (1991) (Microfiche ref.: St Andrew 1 - 9:F12; St Andrew 2 - 5:G9).

Blomefield F *An essay towards a topographical history of the county of Norfolk* (1739/75)

Brett P *Edward Paston (1550-1630): a Norfolk gentleman and his musical collection* Trans. Cambridge Bibliographical Soc. 4, 51-64 (1964)

Bryant T H *The Churches of Norfolk No. CCCCLXXIV S. Andrew's, Thorpe Episcopi*, Norwich Mercury 28 December 1907 and 4 January 1908

Burstall E B *The Pastons and their manor of Binham* Norfolk Archaeology 30, (1952), 101-29

Cannell E F *Norfolk County Mental Hospital – Engineering Department – "The Progress of a Century" 1814-1914* (typescript c.1914)

Carter A *The site of Dussindale* Norfolk Archaeology xxxix, 54-62 (1984)

[Chambers J] *Norfolk Tour* (1829)

Clifford D and Clifford T *John Crome* (1968)

Cotman A M and Hawcroft F W *Old Norwich – A Collection of Paintings, Prints and Drawings of an Ancient City* (1961)

Cozens-Hardy B (editor) *The diary of Sylas Neville, 1767-1788* (1950)

Dodwell B (editor) *The Charters of Norwich Cathedral Priory Part One* (1974)

Eastern Evening News 20 December 1968 and 3 January 1969 (old doorways at Thorpe Lodge and Thorpe Hall) (see also Kent E A and Stephenson A *Norwich Inheritance* (1948))

Ewing W C *Notices of the Norwich merchant's marks* Norfolk Archaeology 3, (1852), 176-228

Farrow M A (editor) *Wills at Norwich 1370-1550* Norfolk Record Soc. 16 (1943-45)

Farrow M A and Barton T F (editors) *Index of wills proved in the Consistory Court of Norwich 1604-1686* Norfolk Record Society 28 (1958)

Fawcett T *Thorpe Water Frolic* Norfolk Archaeology xxxvi, 393-398 (1977)

Goreham G *The history of Thorpe Hamlet, Norwich* unpublished typescript (1964)

Grigor J *The Eastern aboretum; or register of remarkable trees, seats, gardens etc. in the county of Norfolk* (1841)

(Hardy C) *Memories of Norwich and its inhabitants fifty years ago by a nonagenarian* (1888)

Harper-Bill C (editor) *English Episcopal Acta 21 – Norwich 1215-1243* (2000)

Harrison T *Postwick and relatives: written in the early part of the eighteenth century, by T Harrison of Great Plumstead* (1858)

Hayes R *The 'Private Life' of a Late Medieval Bishop: William Alnwick, Bishop of Norwich and Lincoln* in Rogers N (editor) *England in the Fifteenth Century* (1994)

Hughey R (editor) *The correspondence of Lady Katherine Paston 1603-1627* Norfolk Record Society 14 (1941)

Kelly G I *The King's Head Public House, 36 Yarmouth Road, Thorpe St Andrew – A history* (typescript 1987)

Kent E A – *Thorpe Hall* – paper read on Norfolk and Norwich Archaeological Society excursion in July 1927 – Norfolk Archaeology 23, (1928), xlvii- l

Kitson S D *The Life of John Sell Cotman* (1937)

MacCulloch D *A Reformation in the balance: power struggles in the diocese of Norwich, 1533-1553* in Rawcliffe C and others (editors) *Counties and Communities Essays on East Anglian History* (1996)

Marshall W *The Rural Economy of Norfolk* (1787)

Moore A *The Norwich School of Artists* (1985)

Norfolk Chronicle 2 June 1866

Norfolk and Norwich directories - various

Norwich Mercury July 1841, 9 July 1842, 2 June 1866

Pevsner N *The Buildings of England – North-East Norfolk and Norwich* (1962)

Rajnai M *The Norwich School of Painters* (1978)

Roberts V *Notes on the History of St Andrew's Hospital* (typescript c. 1998)

Robinson B and Rose E J *Norfolk Origins 2: Roads and Tracks* (1983)

Rose E J and Davison A J *'St Catherine's Thorpe' - the Birth and Death of a Myth* Norfolk Archaeology xl, 179-181 (1988)

Rye W *Castles and manor houses from the Conquest to the present time* (1916)

Sotherton N *The Commoyson in Norfolk 1549* written circa 1550-1560 (edited edition by Yaxley S, (1987))

Stark J *Scenery of the rivers of Norfolk, comprising the Yare, the Waveney, and the Bure...with historical and geological descriptions (by J W Robberds Esq.)* (1834)

Supple W R *A History of Thorpe-next-Norwich otherwise Thorpe Episcopi and Thorpe S. Andrew* (1917)

Tanner N P (editor) *Heresy trials in the diocese of Norwich, 1423-31* (1977)

Thomson D G *The Norfolk County Asylum, Thorpe, Norwich 1814-1903* (1903)

Thorpe St Andrew Parish Council *Snippets 1895-1995* (1995)

Walpole J *Art and Artists of the Norwich School* (1997)

Williams J F (editor) *Bishop Redman's visitation 1597* Norfolk Record Society 18 (1946)

Williamson T *The Origins of Norfolk* (1993)

Yaxley D and Virgoe N *The Manor House in Norfolk* (1978)

Young A *General View of the Agriculture of the County of Norfolk* (1804)

Maps

Sanctuary map of Norwich of 1541 in Kirkpatrick J. *Streets and lanes of the city of Norwich* (1889)

Cuningham's map of Norwich 1558

Mousehold map of 1585 in Kirkpatrick J. *Streets and lanes of the city of Norwich* (1889)

Mousehold Heath showing sheepwalks, circa 1600 – Norfolk Record Office (NRO) MS 4460

John Kirkpatrick's "Plan of the Churchyard & Precinct of the Chappel of St William in the Wood near Norwich", circa 1720 - in Goulburn E M *A history of Norwich Cathedral, with description of its exterior and interior, tombs, sculptures, paintings, windows* (1880)

Sketch maps of certain tithable land in common field and meadow of between 1700 and 1731- see NRO PD228 below

1767 Plan and survey of River Wensum [Yare] and riparian owners - NRO Case 16e 108/109

Faden's map of Norfolk surveyed 1790-94 and printed 1797, in Barringer J C *An introduction to Faden's map of Norfolk* Norfolk Record Society 42 (1975)

1801 Thorpe enclosure map, showing allotments of Mousehold Heath in NRO N/TC 50/6

circa 1817 Ordnance survey map (sketch map of Norwich)

1824 Map of County and City of Norwich , Woodrow and Newton surveyors – NRO N/TC 62/1

1825 Map of rivers from Norwich to Reedham, with names of owners of adjacent lands – NRO MC 103/47

1841 Thorpe Tithe map with 1842 Tithe apportionment – NRO 596

1861 Enclosure map for Thorpe Low Common with enclosure award – NRO/C/ Sca/292

Ordnance Survey 25 inch maps of the 1880s and later

Manuscript sources in Norfolk Record Office

Rye Manuscripts (4691/80A Z3F) – papers regarding lecture about Thorpe, including note about Counsels' Opinions on rights over green 1757 and 1766.

Rye Manuscripts 6 Norris volumes 2 and 5 (also MF 569-70)

Libellum de mensuracione Bosci de Thorp inter dominum Episcopum et Priorem (DCN 51/111) (14th or 15th century (?) book of measurement of Thorpe Wood)

PD 228 - Parish documents of Thorpe Episcopi or Thorpe-next-Norwich

/39 Glebe terriers 1763-1955

/51 Sequestrators' accounts 1670; Tithe accounts 1700-1731, including two small sketch maps of land in common field and meadow

/76 Churchwardens' accounts and Vestry minutes 1745-1875

/111 Town House (i.e. Church House) Declaration of Trust 1587

/112 Town House: copy of conveyance to new trustees 1704

/114 Papers re sale of Town House

/149 List of owners and tenants of commonages at Thorpe 1741

/151 Thorpe inclosure; settlement of claims 1800; notice under award to John Harvey 1801;letter re boundaries between hamlet and parish 1808

/152 Agreement between Sir Roger Kerrison, John Harvey, Jehoshaphat Postle and other landowners re use of Low Common, 1803

/153 Sale particulars of estate in Thorpe and Carrow 1810; of estate in Thorpe 1815

Abstracts of title including estate of John Harvey deceased 1675-1842 – MC 1940/3, 895x8

Thorpe Lodge sale particulars 1842 – MC 860

Glebe terriers 1621-1753 (DN/TER/148/3/1-32)

Manorial Court Rolls of Thorpe-next-Norwich with Plumstead 1721-1841 (MF/X/163/7 and MF/X/233/7 and 8)

St Andrew's Hospital, Thorpe - records (SAH)

Other Manuscript sources

Census Returns 1841-1901

Norfolk Sites and Monuments Record

Acknowledgements

I would particularly like to thank Miss Janet Smith of the Thorpe History Group for her constant support and encouragement and as an unerring supplier of information. I am also grateful to Mrs Vivienne Roberts (also of the Thorpe History Group) for her help and information, particularly about St Andrew's Hospital and Octagon Cottage.

I would also like to thank Mr Brian Larkman for drawing Maps I to VII and the map reproduced as Plate 32 in Appendix 2.

I have written this book at intervals over a period of about 7 years. During this time, I have been grateful for the assistance of the staff of the Norfolk County Council Library and Information Service and the Norfolk Record Office. I have also appreciated the help of members of the staff of Norfolk Landscape Archaeology, the keepers and maintainers of the Norfolk Sites and Monument Record at Gressenhall.

I am grateful to all those who have supplied me with photographs for this book. Several of them are from my own postcard collection. The original provenance of some of them has been difficult to establish. Plates 4, 11, 12, 16, 22 and 28 have been reproduced by courtesy of the Norfolk County Council Library and Information Service. Plates 5, 17 and 26 have been reproduced by courtesy of Mrs Vivienne Roberts. Plate 14 has been reproduced by courtesy of the Norwich Castle Museum & Art Gallery. The map reproduced as Plate 31 in Appendix 2 has been included by courtesy of the Norfolk Record Office and is part of a map described by them as "Mousehold Heath showing sheepwalks, circa 1600".

Trevor Nuthall